Mike McGrath

CSS

Fourth Edition

In easy steps is an imprint of In Easy Steps Limited
16 Hamilton Terrace · Holly Walk · Leamington Spa
Warwickshire · United Kingdom · CV32 4LY
www.ineasysteps.com

Fourth Edition

In Easy Steps Limited supports The Forest Stewardship Council (FSC),
the leading international forest certification organization. All our titles
that are printed on Greenpeace approved FSC certified paper carry the
FSC logo.

MIX
Paper from
responsible sources
FSC® C020837

Printed and bound in the United Kingdom

ISBN 978-1-84078-875-4

Contents

How to Use This Book

The examples in this book demonstrate CSS features that are supported by leading web browsers, and the screenshots illustrate the actual results produced by the listed code examples. Certain colorization conventions are used to clarify the code listed in the steps...

CSS selectors, properties, and punctuation are colored blue, but specified values are colored red:

div > span { color : Red ; background : Yellow ; }

CSS and HTML comments are colored green: /* CSS comment */ <!-- HTML comment -->

HTML tags are colored blue, literal text and JavaScript code is colored black, and element attribute values are colored orange in both HTML and CSS code:

<p class="frame">CSS in easy steps</p>

p.frame { color : White ; background : Green ; }

Additionally, in order to identify each source code file described in the steps, a file icon and file name appears in the margin alongside the steps:

page.html   style.css   image.png   cursor.cur   data.xml   script.pl

The source code of HTML documents used in the book's examples is not listed in full to avoid unnecessary repetition but the listed HTML code is the entire fragment of the document to which the listed CSS code is applied. You can download a single ZIP archive file containing all the example files by following these easy steps:

1 Browse to **www.ineasysteps.com** then navigate to Free Resources and choose the Downloads section

2 Find CSS in easy steps, 4th edition in the list, then click on the hyperlink entitled All Code Examples to download the archive

3 Now, extract the archive contents to any convenient location on your computer

If you don't achieve the result illustrated in any example, simply compare your code to that in the original example files you have downloaded to discover where you went wrong.

1 Get Started in CSS

Meet CSS

Cascading Style Sheets (CSS) is a language used to control the presentation of elements within HyperText Markup Language (HTML) documents. Presentation is specified by "styles" that may be assigned "inline" to HTML element **style** attributes, or by "rules" within **<style> </style>** tags in the HTML document's head section, or as rules within separate style sheets. Each style rule selects specified elements then applies specified styles to them.

CSS was created by the World Wide Web Consortium (W3C) to regain control of document markup as HTML grew from the initial few "tags" that merely defined the structural elements of a document – headings, paragraphs, hyperlinks, lists, etc. As further tags were added controlling images, text color, font size and background color, it became recognized that the source code of many web pages often contained a great deal of markup for very little actual content.

The W3C offered a solution to regain control of document markup by separating their structural and presentational aspects. HTML tags would continue to control the structure but presentational aspects would now be controlled by "style rules" written in the Cascading Style Sheets (CSS) language. Besides distinguishing between structural and presentational aspects of a document, the CSS solution brings these additional benefits:

The W3C is an international consortium whose members work together to develop web standards. The CSS home page can be found on the W3C website at **www.w3.org/Style/CSS**

- **Easier maintenance** – a single style sheet can control multiple HTML documents, so changing appearance across an entire website is possible by editing just one style sheet.

- **Smaller file sizes** – removal of all presentational markup from HTML produces smaller files, which download faster.

- **Greater control** – margins, borders, padding, background color and background images to any HTML element, and the appearance of certain parts of the interface, such as the cursor, can now be specified.

The latest CSS specification (CSS3) is divided into modules that allow enhancements such as rounded borders, drop-shadows, gradient color-fills and animation effects – these and more are demonstrated by example in this book.

The term "Cascading" in CSS describes the manner in which style rules can fall from one style sheet to another. The cascade determines which style rule will have precedence over others and be the one applied to the selected HTML element.

There are three basic types of style sheet that can specify style rules to be applied to HTML elements:

● **Browser (default) style sheet** – browsers employ an intrinsic set of style rules that they apply to all web pages by default. These vary slightly between different browsers but all have common features such as black text and blue hyperlinks.

● **User style sheet** – some browsers allow the user to specify their own appearance preferences, which effectively creates a custom style sheet that overrides the browser's default style sheet.

● **Author style sheet** – where the HTML document specifies a style sheet created by the web page author, the browser will apply the style rules it contains, overriding both the user style sheet and the default browser style sheet.

CSS is the universally accepted style sheet language that is recognized by all modern web browsers.

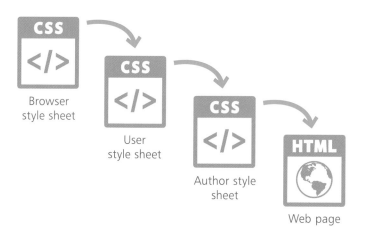

Browser style sheet

User style sheet

Author style sheet

Web page

Final precedence of style rules that target the same element is determined by their "specificity" weight – see pages 22/23.

So the cascade means that the browsers will typically apply the style rules in an author style sheet, if present, otherwise it will apply the style rules in a user style sheet, if present, otherwise it will apply the style rules in the browser's style sheet by default.

Create Rules

In CSS each style rule is comprised of two main parts:

1 **Selector** – specifying which element/s of the HTML document are the target of that rule.

2 **Declaration Block** – specifying how properties of the selected target element should be styled.

A style rule (or "style rule set") begins with the selector, followed by the declaration block within a pair of curly brackets (braces). The braces contain one or more declarations that each specify a property and a valid value for that property, as in this example:

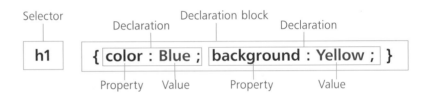

Typically, the selector targets (selects) a particular HTML element for styling – such as all **<h1>** heading elements in the document using the style rules example above.

The declaration block in the example above contains two declarations to specify the foreground and background colors of the selected target elements. The CSS **color** property is assigned a **Blue** value – so each **<h1>** heading element will have blue foreground text. Similarly, the CSS **background** property is assigned a **Yellow** value – so each **<h1>** heading element will have a yellow background.

Notice how the CSS declaration uses a : colon character to assign a value to a property. Notice also that each declaration is terminated by a ; semi-colon character.

Strictly speaking, the final declaration in the declaration block does not need to be terminated by a semi-colon but most web page authors prefer to habitually terminate all CSS declarations – so they need not remember to add a separating semi-colon when adding further declarations to an existing style rule set.

Hot tip

The **background** property is a "shorthand" property for **background-color** and several other CSS properties that are described on page 26.

10

1 When creating a new CSS style rule, the author must initially specify a selector to target the HTML element to which the rule will be applied – the CSS selector is everything that appears before the opening brace of the declaration block
h1

rules.html

2 Next, the declaration block must be created by adding a pair of braces after the selector
h1 {   }

3 Now, a declaration can be inserted within the declaration block to assign a value to a property
h1 { color : Blue ; }

Whitespace (spaces, tabs, line feeds, and carriage returns) is permitted within style rules to allow the author to format the style rules to their own preference.

4 A second declaration can then be added within the declaration block, separated from the first by a semi-colon
h1 { color : Blue ; background : Yellow ; }

5 The style rule set is now complete but can also be applied to another HTML element by extending the selector to become a comma-separated list
h1, h2 { color : Blue ; background : Yellow ; }

6 Further style rule sets can then be added below the first style rule set to target other elements
h1, h2   { color : Blue ; background : Yellow ; }
p   { color : Red ; }

Style rule sets with fewer than four declarations are written on a single line, otherwise they are written across multiple lines for clarity – typically the selector and **{** opening brace will appear on the first line, followed by declarations on individual lines, then the **}** closing brace on the final line. Code is listed in this book more concisely formatted due to limited page space.

Apply Rules

A style sheet is simply a collection of style rules to be applied to an HTML document. An internal style sheet can be created by inserting the style rules between **<style>** and **</style>** tags in the head section of the HTML document.

Additionally, the head section of each HTML document should include a **<meta>** tag to set up the "viewport" for the page. This tag determines the visible area of the web page to suit the device on which the page is being viewed, and looks exactly like this:

```
<meta  name="viewport"
       content="width=device-width, initial-scale=1.0" >
```

The viewport's **<meta>** tag does not need to be spread across two lines. It is shown like that here due to space constraints.

- The **width=device-width** part sets the width of the page to match the screen-width of the viewing device.

- The **initial-scale=1.0** part sets the initial zoom level of the browser to 100% when the web page is first loaded.

apply.html

1 Open a plain text editor (such as Windows' Notepad app) then create an HTML document containing heading, sub-heading, and paragraph elements
```
<!DOCTYPE HTML>
<html lang="en">
<head>
<meta charset="UTF-8">
<meta  name="viewport"
       content="width=device-width, initial-scale=1.0" >
<title>Apply Style Rules</title>
<!-- Internal style sheet to be inserted here. -->
</head>
<body>
<h1>Heading</h1>
<h2>Sub-heading</h2>
<p>Paragraph </p>
</body>
</html>
```

2 In the document's head section, insert an internal style sheet containing style rules for the heading element
```
<style>
h1      { color : Blue ;  background : Yellow ; }
</style>
```

3 Save the HTML file then open it in your web browser to see the internal style sheet rules applied to the heading

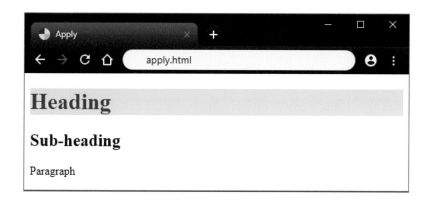

Style rules can also be applied by assigning "inline" properties and values to the **style** attribute of an element:

4 Edit the sub-heading tag to add an inline rule set
<h2 style="color : White ; background : Green ;" >

Style rules can also be applied from an external style sheet:

5 Open a plain text editor, then type the style rules below and save it as an external style sheet named "external.css"
p { color : Yellow ; background : Red ; }

6 Edit the HTML file to link the external style sheet by inserting this tag in the document's head section
<link rel="stylesheet" href="external.css" type="text/css">

7 Save the HTML file then reopen it in your web browser to see the inline and external style sheet rules applied

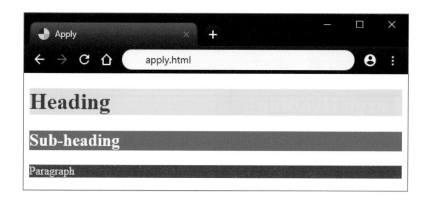

Inline rules may override rules specified by other style sheets, as inline rules are the last to be applied by the browser.

external.css

13

External style sheets are great to maintain consistent styles across multiple web pages, so authors can change a single rule that will be instantly applied across all pages. Internal style sheets are used by most examples in this book so that each HTML document is a standalone example.

Select Type

The selector part of a style rule selects elements in an HTML document to be styled according to the values specified in that rule's declaration block.

A "type" selector selects all elements in the page that match the selector. Multiple elements can be selected by a type selector that specifies a comma-separated list of element types.

type.html

1 Create an HTML document containing a heading and an unordered list of hyperlinks within a division container
```
<div>
<h1>Large Heading</h1>
<ul>
<li><a href="https://google.com">Google</a></li>
<li><a href="https://yahoo.com">Yahoo</a></li>
<li><a href="https://mediafire.com">MediaFire</a></li>
</ul>
</div>
```

2 Add a style sheet with a style rule setting the width of the container element at half the page width
```
<style>
div { width : 50% ; }
</style>
```

3 Add style rules setting the background color of all hyperlinks, the heading, and list elements
```
a { background : Yellow ; }
h1, ul { color: White ; background : Blue ; }
```

4 Save the HTML file then open the web page in a browser to see the elements styled by type selectors

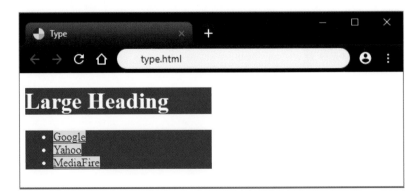

Beware

Remember that there must be a comma between the element types in a selector targeting multiple element types.

14

The CSS * universal selector can be used to select elements of all types within an HTML document – as if it was a selector listing all element types as a comma-separated list:

5 Add a style rule with a universal selector to make all text italic, then save the HTML file again and refresh the browser to see both heading and list text become italic
* { font-style : italic ; }

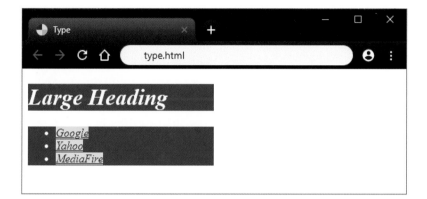

You will discover many more CSS font properties in Chapter 3 of this book.

The * universal selector can also be used to select elements of any type contained within a specified element type:

6 Add a style rule with a universal selector to add a 2-pixel wide border around all elements within the "div" container, then save the HTML file once more and refresh the browser to see borders around the elements
div * { border : 2px solid Red ; }

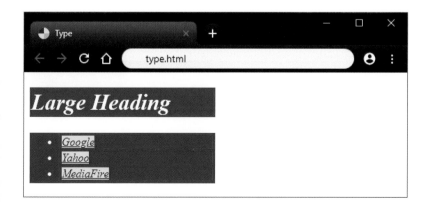

The **div *** selector selects elements of all types within the div container, but not the **<div>** element itself.

Select Class

As an alternative to selecting elements by type, a class selector can select HTML elements that contain a **class** attribute that has been assigned a value matching the selector. The class selector begins with a . period character followed by the **class** value to match. This is especially useful to apply the style rule across a number of specific elements of different type.

Additionally, a class selector can be combined with a type selector to select specific instances of a class. In this case, the selector first specifies the element type, followed by a . period character and the **class** value to match:

class.html

1. Create an HTML document containing a paragraph and two spanned words – which all have a common **class** value
```
<p class="frame">You can fool all the people
<span class="frame">some</span> of the time, and
<span class="frame">some</span> of the people all the
time, but you cannot fool all the people all the time.</p>
```

2. Add a style sheet with a style rule drawing red borders around each element using the **class** value
```
<style>
.frame { border : 2px solid Red ; }
</style>
```

3. Now, add a style rule overriding the previous one for the paragraph element only – to draw a blue border around the paragraph and to set its width
```
p.frame { border : 2px solid Blue ; width : 50% ; }
```

4. Save the HTML document then open the web page in a browser to see elements styled by the class selectors

16

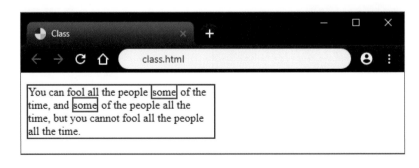

Select Identity

Similar to a class selector, an identity selector can select HTML elements that contain an **id** attribute that has been assigned a value matching the selector. The identity selector begins with a **#** hash character followed by the **id** value to match. This is mostly useful to apply the style rule to one specific element, as each **id** attribute value must be unique within the HTML document.

Optionally, an identity selector can be combined with a type selector simply to identify the element type. In this case, the selector first specifies the element type, followed by a hash character and the **id** value to match:

1. Create an HTML document containing a paragraph and two spanned phrases – which all have a unique **id** value
```
<p id="para1">You may only be someone
<span id="span1">in the world</span><br>
but to someone else you may
<span id="span2">be the world</span></p>
```

identity.html

2. Add a style sheet with style rules painting colored backgrounds behind the text in each **span** element
```
<style>
#span1 { color : White ; background : Yellow ; }
#span2 { color : White ; background : Green ; }
</style>
```

Hot tip

3. Now, add a style rule to paint a colored background behind the rest of the paragraph and to set its width
```
p#para1 { background : Yellow ; width : 70% ; }
```

4. Save the HTML document then open the web page in a browser to see elements styled by the identity selectors

If a class selector and an identity selector both attempt to style the same property of one element, the identity selector value would be applied as it has greater importance. See page 22 for more on how selectors rate importance.

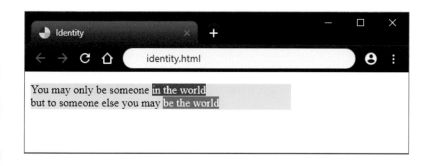

Select Relatives

In addition to selecting target elements by type, class or identity (as described on pages 14-17), CSS allows selectors to be combined to select elements relative to other elements in the HTML document. These "combinators" provide four options:

Descendant Selector (*space*)

This selects all elements that are descendants of a parent element. The CSS selector first specifies the parent element, then a space, followed by the descendant element. For example, to select all **\<p\>** paragraph elements within a **\<div\>** division element <u>at any level</u> of descendancy:

div p { }

Child Selector (>)

This selects all elements that are children of a parent element. The CSS selector first specifies the parent element, then a > angled bracket character, followed by the child element. For example, to select all **\<p\>** paragraph elements whose <u>direct parent</u> is a **\<div\>** division element:

div > p { }

Adjacent Sibling Selector (+)

This selects all elements that are adjacent siblings immediately following a parent element. The CSS selector first specifies the parent element, then a + plus character, followed by the sibling element. For example, to select all **\<p\>** paragraph elements that are placed <u>immediately after</u> each **\<div\>** division element:

div + p { }

General Sibling Selector (~)

This selects all elements that are siblings immediately following a parent element. The CSS selector first specifies the parent element, then a ~ tilde character, followed by the sibling element. For example, to select all **\<p\>** paragraph elements that <u>follow</u> a **\<div\>** division element:

div ~ p { }

You can specify more than one descendant to further refine a descendant selector, such as **div p span { }**.

18

A child selector will target all child elements of the parent – even if there are other element levels between them.

Sibling elements must have the same parent. Adjacent siblings must immediately follow the parent element, but general siblings are all those contained directly within the parent.

1 Create an HTML document containing a heading, several divisions and paragraphs, plus an aside element

relative.html

```
<h3>Heading</h3>
<div>Content</div> <div>More content</div>

<div>    <p>Para 1</p> <p>Para 2</p>
        <aside> <p>Para 3</p> </aside>
</div>
```

2 Add a style sheet with style rules selecting all paragraphs, and only the division element that immediately follows the heading element

```
<style>
div p { color : White ; background : Blue ; }
h3 + div { background : Yellow ; }
</style>
```

3 Save the HTML document then open the web page in a browser to see elements styled by the relative selectors

Adjacent sibling

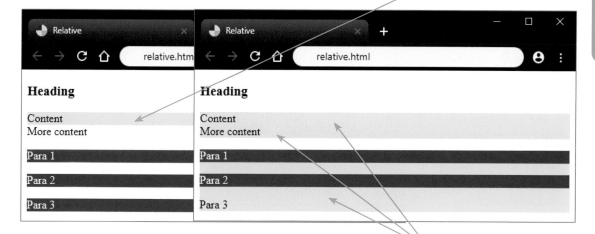

General siblings

4 Edit the style rules to select only paragraphs whose direct parent is a division element, and all division elements that follow the heading element

```
div > p { color : White ; background : Blue ; }
h3 ~ div { background : Yellow ; }
```

5 Save the HTML document once more, then refresh the browser to see the changes

Select Attributes

In addition to selecting target elements by type, class, identity or by relationship (as described on pages 14-19), CSS selectors can target HTML elements that have specific attributes or particular attribute values. Attribute selectors have seven options:

Attribute Name Selector [*attribute*]
This selects all elements that have a specified attribute, by stating an element followed by an attribute name in [ ] brackets:

ol[*attribute*]

Attribute Value Selector [*attribute="value"*]
This selects all elements that have a specified attribute and a specified value, stated within the [ ] brackets:

li[class="*value*"]

Attribute Value Item Selector [*attribute~="value"*]
This selects all elements that have a specified attribute and a list of values that contain a specified word:

li[class~="*item*"]

Attribute First Word Selector [*attribute|="value"*]
This selects all elements that have a specified attribute and a value that begins with a specified word:

li[class|="*word*"]

Attribute Substring Selector [*attribute*="value"*]
This selects all elements that have a specified attribute and a value that includes a specified substring anywhere in a value or list:

li[class*="*substring*"]

Attribute First Substring Selector [*attribute^="value"*]
This selects all elements that have a specified attribute and a value that begins with a specified substring anywhere in a value or list:

li[class^="*substring*"]

Attribute Final Substring Selector [*attribute$="value"*]
This selects all elements that have a specified attribute and a value that ends with a specified substring anywhere in a value or list:

li[class$="*substring*"]

Beware

The first word selector will only select the element if the attribute value is a single whole word or hyphenated – for example, selecting **[class="top"]** with values of "topcat", or "top-cat".

...cont'd

1 Create an HTML document containing an ordered list in which all elements include attributes

```
<ol id="list">
<li class="reptile">Alligator</li>
<li class="domestic animal">Dog</li>
<li class="animal wild">Tiger</li>
<li class="cat-family">Lion</li>
<li class="sea fish">Barracuda</li>
<li class="topcat">Cartoon</li>
<li class ="domestic bird">Budgerigar</li>
</ol>
```

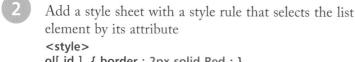

attribute.html

2 Add a style sheet with a style rule that selects the list element by its attribute

```
<style>
ol[ id ]  { border : 2px solid Red ; }
</style>
```

3 Now, add style rules that select all the list items by their attribute values

```
li[class="reptile"]       { background : Red ; }
li[class~="animal"]       { background : Blue ; }
li[ class|="cat" ]        { background : Green ; }
li[class*="fi"]           { background : Yellow ; }
li[class^="top"]          { background : Orange ; }
li[class$="ird"]          { background : Purple ; }
```

The value specified to the three substring selectors does not need to be a whole word.

4 Save the HTML document then open the web page in a browser to see elements styled by the attribute selectors

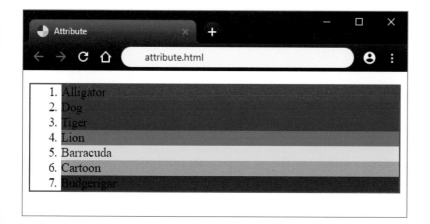

Weigh Importance

Where more than one style rule targets properties of the same element, the CSS cascade evaluates their importance by examining their selector's "specificity" – to consider how specifically each one targets the element to determine their relative importance.

There are four categories that define the importance of a selector. These are, in descending order of importance, as follows:

Don't forget

Embedded style sheet rules take precedence over those in external style sheets, and the * universal selector has a zero specificity value of **0,0,0,0**.

- **Inline**: a style rule declared to the **style** attribute directly within an element – for example, **style="color:White;"**.

- **Identity**: a selector that targets the **id** attribute of an element – for example, **h2#header**.

- **Class, Attribute**: a selector that targets the **class** or [*attribute*] of an element – for example, **h2.head**.

- **Element**: a selector that targets the type of an element by name – for example, **h2**.

The specificity evaluation process awards points for each selector component, which get stored in four weight "registers" for later comparison against the specificity value of conflicting selectors. So the specificity value can be expressed as a comma-separated list – in which **0,0,0,0** is a zero specificity value. The selector component points are awarded like this:

- For inline **style** attribute declarations, add **1,0,0,0**.

- For each **id** attribute in the selector, add **0,1,0,0**.

- For each **class** attribute in the selector or attribute value selection, add **0,0,1,0**.

- For each element (or pseudo-element) in the selector, add **0,0,0,1**.

If two selectors have the same specificity weight rating, the "latest rule counts" so the lower rule in the style sheet will be applied.

Hot tip

Pseudo elements are described on page 72.

1 Create an HTML document containing three headings

```
<h2 style="color:White;" >Element Style</h2>

<h2 id="header">Identity Style</h2>

<h2 class="head">Class Style</h2>
```

specificity.html

2 Add a style sheet with a style rule that selects all heading elements by type

```
<style>
h2 { color : Yellow ; }
</style>
```

3 Now, add style rules that each target the heading elements' background property in different ways

```
h2       { background : Red ; }      /* 0,0,0,1 */
body h2 { background : Blue ; }      /* 0,0,0,2 */

#header    { background : Green ; }  /* 0,1,0,0 */
h2#header { background : Red ; }      /* 0,1,0,1 */

h2.head        { background : Red ; }   /* 0,0,1,1 */
body h2.head { background : Green ; } /* 0,0,1,2 */
```

Hot tip

The /* */ syntax may be used to add single and multi-line comments within a CSS style sheet.

4 Save the HTML document then open the web page in a browser to see the elements styled after considering specificity to rate their importance

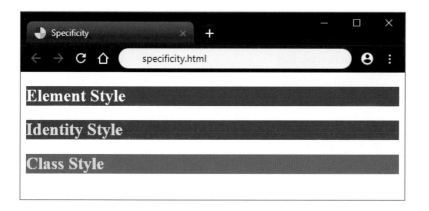

Hot tip

See that the first heading's color is applied from the inline declaration – overriding the type selector in the style sheet. Each heading's background is applied by the rule with most weight points.

24

Paint Colors

Web browsers recognize all the color names listed in these tables. You can use these names in CSS rules to set the color of HTML elements. The names are not case-sensitive so they may also be written in all lowercase letters – for example, **background : aqua ;**.

Hot tip

Colors can also be written as the Red, Green, Blue components that make up the color – for example, the color red is **rgb(255, 0, 0)**. Alternatively, colors can be written as hexadecimal numbers – for example, the color red is hexadecimal **#FF0000**, which is Red **FF** (decimal 255), **00** (decimal 0) Green, and **00** (decimal 0) Blue.

AliceBlue	AntiqueWhite	Aqua
Aquamarine	Azure	Beige
Bisque	Black	BlanchedAlmond
Blue	BlueViolet	Brown
BurlyWood	CadetBlue	Chartreuse
Chocolate	Coral	CornflowerBlue
Cornsilk	Crimson	Cyan
DarkBlue	DarkCyan	DarkGoldenRod
DarkGray	DarkGreen	DarkKhaki
DarkMagenta	DarkOliveGreen	DarkOrange
DarkOrchid	DarkRed	DarkSalmon
DarkSeaGreen	DarkSlateBlue	DarkSlateGray
DarkTurquoise	DarkViolet	DeepPink
DeepSkyBlue	DimGray	DodgerBlue
FireBrick	FloralWhite	ForestGreen
Fuchsia	Gainsboro	GhostWhite
Gold	GoldenRod	Gray
Green	GreenYellow	HoneyDew
HotPink	IndianRed	Indigo
Ivory	Khaki	Lavender
LavenderBlush	LawnGreen	LemonChiffon
LightBlue	LightCoral	LightCyan

LightGoldenRodYellow	LightGray	LightGreen
LightPink	LightSalmon	LightSeaGreen
LightSkyBlue	LightSlateGray	LightSteelBlue
LightYellow	Lime	LimeGreen
Linen	Magenta	Maroon
MediumAquamarine	MediumBlue	MediumOrchid
MediumPurple	MediumSeaGreen	MediumSlateBlue
MediumSpringGreen	MediumTurquoise	MediumVioletRed
MidnightBlue	MintCream	MistyRose
Moccasin	NavajoWhite	Navy
OldLace	Olive	OliveDrab
Orange	OrangeRed	Orchid
PaleGoldenRod	PaleGreen	PaleTurquoise
PaleVioletRed	PapayaWhip	PeachPuff
Peru	Pink	Plum
PowderBlue	Purple	RebeccaPurple
Red	RosyBrown	RoyalBlue
SaddleBrown	Salmon	SandyBrown
SeaGreen	SeaShell	Sienna
Silver	SkyBlue	SlateBlue
SlateGray	Snow	SpringGreen
SteelBlue	Tan	Teal
Thistle	Tomato	Turquoise
Violet	Wheat	White
WhiteSmoke	Yellow	YellowGreen

Hot tip

Colors can also be written as their Hue, Saturation, Lightness (HSL) values – for example, the color full red is specified as **hsl(0, 100%, 50%)**.

Hot tip

Optionally, a fourth Alpha value can be added to the color specification to determine the opacity of the color – for example, a half-transparent full red color specified as **rgba(255, 0, 0, 0.5)** or as **hsla(0, 100%, 50%, 0.5)**.

Set Backgrounds

Just as each element can have a background color specified to its **background** property, a background image can be specified to its **background** property, as a **url(*filename*)** value. Here, the *filename* is the path to an image file – for example, **background : url(bg.png)** ;.

The **background** property can also be used to specify both a background image and color as space-separated values – for example, **background : LightBlue url(bg.png)** ;. Background images are placed on a layer above the background's color layer so specifying an image with transparent areas will allow the background color to shine through the image.

Any specified background image will normally be positioned at the top-left corner of the element and the browser will, by default, repeatedly "tile" the image row-by-row across the element area. This behavior can be modified by assigning different values to the **background** property where values of **repeat-x** restricts the tiling pattern to one horizontal row and **repeat-y** restricts the tiling pattern to one vertical column. Tiling can also be prevented by assigning a **no-repeat** value so that a single copy of the image appears at the top-left corner of the content box.

The position of a background image can be specified to the **background** property to control its horizontal position with values of **left**, **center**, and **right**, and to control its vertical position with values of **top, center**, and **bottom**. Combining horizontal and vertical values together with a **no-repeat** value lets you set a single version of the image at a given position within the element area – for example, **background : url(bg.png) no-repeat top right** ;.

The **background** property has a **scroll** value by default that relates to the viewport, not the element, so by default a background image will scroll along with the page. Should you prefer to attach a background page image, so it does not scroll along with the page, you can specify a **fixed** value to the **background** property so the background image will remain at a specified position relative to the viewport when the page gets scrolled.

All background values can be specified in a space-separated list to the **background** shorthand property, or individually to properties of **background-color, background-image, background-repeat, background-position** and **background-attachment**.

...cont'd

1 Create an HTML document containing two paragraphs
```
<p class="repeat"></p>
<p class="repeat-y"></p>
```

background.html

2 Add a style sheet with rules that set the dimensions and background properties of each paragraph
```
<style>
p.repeat { width : 384px ; height : 128px ;
 background : LightBlue url( crab.png ) ; }

p.repeat-y { width : 384px ; height : 128px ; background :
DeepSkyBlue url( crab.png ) repeat-y top right ;  }
</style>
```

3 Now, add a style rule that attaches a background image to the page at a fixed position
```
body { background : url( crab.png )
        no-repeat bottom right fixed ; }
```

crab.png – 64px x 64px
Gray areas are transparent.

4 Save the HTML document, then open the web page in a browser to see the backgrounds – scroll the page to see the fixed page background image

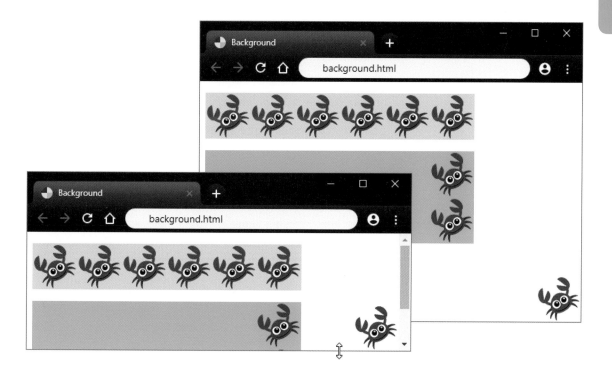

Summary

- CSS is a language provided by the W3C to regain control of markup by separating document structure from presentation.

- The cascade allows style rules to fall from one style sheet to another and determines which style rule will be applied.

- Each style rule comprises a selector and a declaration block.

- Each declaration specifies a property and a value to be applied to that property – separated by a : colon character.

- A style rule set may contain multiple declarations – each terminated by a ; semicolon character.

- Style rules can be specified in an internal style sheet, inline to an HTML element's **style** attribute, or in an external style sheet.

- Type selectors select all elements that match the selector.

- Class selectors select all elements that contain a **class** attribute that has been assigned a value matching the selector.

- Identity selectors select all elements that contain an **id** attribute that has been assigned a value matching the selector.

- Relative selectors are combinators that select elements relative to other elements as descendants, children, or siblings.

- Attribute selectors select elements that have specific attributes or particular attribute values.

- The cascade evaluates the selector's specificity to rate importance by how specifically each one targets the element.

- Color values can be specified by name, hexadecimal value, Red Green Blue value or Hue, Saturation, Lightness value.

- The background shorthand property can specify an element's background color, image, repeat, position, and attachment.

2 Manage the Box Model

Recognize Boxes

Block-level content boxes are, by default, stacked on the page one below another. **Inline** content boxes appear inside a block-level box, one behind another.

Content on a web page is displayed in a number of invisible rectangular boxes that are generated by the browser. These content boxes may be either "block level" or "inline".

Block-level content boxes normally have line breaks before and after the box, such as paragraph, heading, and division elements.

Inline content boxes, on the other hand, do not add line breaks but are simply created within lines of content, such as span, emphasis, and hyperlink elements.

Each block-level content box comprises a core content area surrounded by optional areas for padding, border, and margins:

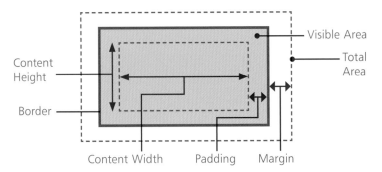

Content is the area filled by text or images. **Padding** is a transparent area around the content. **Border** surrounds the content and padding. **Margin** is a transparent area outside the border.

Style rules can specify values for the **padding, border**, and **margin** properties to control the appearance of content boxes. These all apply to block-level boxes but some properties, such as **width** and **height**, do not apply to inline boxes. Additionally, the **margin** and **padding** properties of inline boxes only apply to either side of the content – not the areas above and below the content.

When the **padding, border**, and **margin** properties all have a zero width, the content box will be the same size as the content area, determined by the dimensions of the content.

Any **padding, border**, and **margin** areas that have a non-zero width are added outside the content area, so the content size remains the same but the box size increases.

The **padding** property extends the area around the content and inherits the background color of the content area. The **border** property extends the area around the content and any padding. The **margin** property extends the area around the content, any padding, and any border, with a transparent background.

...cont'd

1 Create an HTML document with four simple paragraphs, three with assigned class attribute values
```
<p>Content Box</p>
<p class="pad">Content + Padding</p>
<p class="pad bdr">Content + Padding + Border</p>
<p class="pad bdr mgn">
        Content + Padding + Border + Margin</p>
```

box.html

2 Add a style sheet with a rule that sets the background color of the core content area and its width at 300 pixels
```
p { background : MistyRose ; width : 300px ; }
```

3 Next, add a style rule to add padding of 10 pixels around all sides of the content
```
p.pad { padding : 10px ; }
```

4 Now, add a style rule to add a border of 5 pixels around all sides of the padded content area
```
p.bdr { border : 5px solid Tomato ; }
```

5 Finally, add a style rule to add a margin of 20 pixels around all sides of the border
```
p.mgn { margin : 20px ; }
```

6 Save the HTML document then open the web page in a browser to see the content boxes with added padding, borders, and margin

Don't forget

The HTML **<style>** and **</style>** tags are omitted from the steps in all further examples to save book page space. Instructions on how to add style sheets to an HTML document are provided on pages 12-13.

31

Beware

If you specify the width and height of an element you only set the width and height of the content area. You must add any padding, border, and margin areas to calculate the total space occupied by the element. In this case, the total width occupied by the element is **300px** (width) + **20px** (left and right padding) + **10px** (left and right border) + **40px** (left and right margin) = 370 pixels.

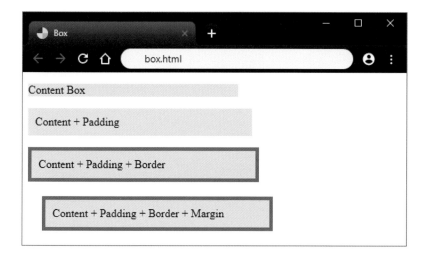

Display Inline

A web page relies upon the creation of block-level content boxes, to determine its general layout, and the creation of inline content boxes within the blocks to determine its precise layout.

This places great emphasis on whether an element is considered block-level or inline to determine the display format. Generally, the default display format for each element will be the most appropriate. For example, it's generally desirable to display list items on individual lines in a block-level list.

The display format of an element can also be explicitly determined by a style rule that assigns the **block** or **inline** keywords to that element's **display** property. This means that content can be displayed in a different format without changing the HTML tags. For example, list items can be displayed on a single line with a **display : inline ;** declaration.

Additionally, an inline content-box can have its **display** property assigned an **inline-block** value to allow it to be displayed somewhat like a block-level content box. The inline-block still appears inline, as usual, but unlike regular inline content boxes its **width** and **height** properties can be assigned values to control its size.

Assigning a non-default display type to an element only changes the way it gets displayed – in the document tree inline elements are always descendants of block-level elements.

List items can be made to display horizontally, rather than vertically, if each list item element is made into an inline-block. This is often used to create a navigation bar of horizontal links – see page 90.

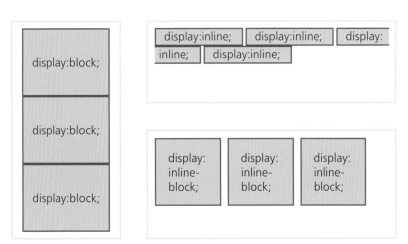

With a **display:inline ;** declaration, top and bottom margins and paddings are not applied – but they are with inline-blocks. Additionally, note that a **display : block ;** declaration will add a line break after the element – but inline-blocks will not.

1 Create an HTML document with three unordered lists

```
<ul class="block">
        <li>Block</li><li>Block</li><li>Block</li></ul>
<ul class="inline" >
        <li>Inline</li><li>Inline</li><li>Inline</li></ul>
<ul class="inline-block" >
<li>Inline Block</li><li>Inline Block</li><li>Inline Block</li>
</ul>
```

display.html

2 Add a style sheet with rules to style each list's border and list item elements

```
ul      { border : 2px solid Tomato ; }
ul > li { background : MistyRose ; margin : 10px ;
          padding : 5px ; width : 100px ; height : 20px ; }
```

3 Now, add style rules to specify the display type for each list's item elements

```
ul.block > li { display : block ; }
ul.inline > li { display : inline ; }
ul.inline-block > li { display : inline-block ; }
```

4 Save the HTML document then open the web page in a browser to see the content displayed in specific formats

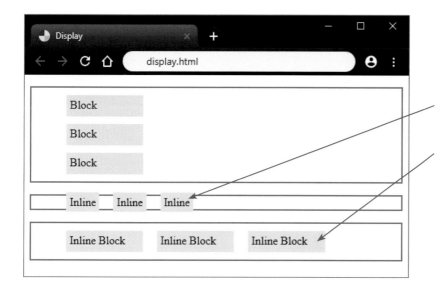

Beware

Inline boxes will not include top and padding or margin values.
Inline Block boxes will include top and padding or margin values.

33

Define Dimensions

When assigning any non-zero value to a property, the declaration must include a two-letter unit name to specify which unit of measurement to apply. The CSS specification provides the following unit names representing real world measurement:

Unit:	Description:	Example:
in (inches)	American standard unit of length measurement	div { width : 1in ; }
cm (centimeters)	Metric unit of length where 2.54 centimeters is equivalent to 1 inch	div { height : 2.54cm ; }
mm (millimeters)	Metric unit of length (one tenth of one centimeter) where 25.4 millimeters is equivalent to 1 inch	div { height : 25.4mm ; }
pt (points)	Typographical unit of font height where 72 points is equivalent to 1 inch	div { font-size : 12pt ; }
pc (picas)	Typographical unit of font height where 6 picas is equivalent to 1 inch	div { font-size : 2pc ; }

The CSS specification also provides the following unit names representing relative values according to the viewing device:

Unit:	Description:	Example:
em (font size)	Abstract typographical unit of font size where 1em is equivalent to the height of a given font	div { font-size : 12pt ; } (1em = 12pt)
ex (font size)	Abstract typographical unit of font size where 1ex is equivalent to the height of lowercase "x" in a font (often 50% of 1em)	div { font-size : 12pt ; } (1ex = 6pt)
px (pixels)	Abstract unit representing the dots on a computer monitor where there are 1024 pixels on each line when the monitor resolution is 1024x768	div { height : 100px ; }

Zero values can be assigned using just a "0" number – without specifying a unit name.

A percentage value can also specify a relative size – where a value of 50% makes the target element half the size of its containing element.

…cont'd

① Create an HTML document containing four division
elements
```
<div id="absolute">3in x &half;in</div>
<div id="container">400px x 150px
  <div id="percent">50% x 50%</div>
  <div id="relative">20em x 2em</div>
</div>
```

dimensions.html

② Add a style sheet with rules to size an element by
absolute units
```
div#absolute { width : 3in ; height : 0.5in ;
                          background : Tomato ; }
```

③ Next, add rules to size an element by monitor resolution
```
div#container { width : 400px ; height : 150px ;
                          background : MistyRose ; }
```

④ Now, add rules to size an element by percentage
```
div#percent { width : 50% ; height : 50% ;
                          background : Tomato ; }
```

⑤ Then, add rules to size an element relative to font height
```
div#relative { width : 20em ; height : 2em ;
                          background : LightSalmon ; }
```

⑥ Save the HTML document then open the web page in a
browser to see the element sizes

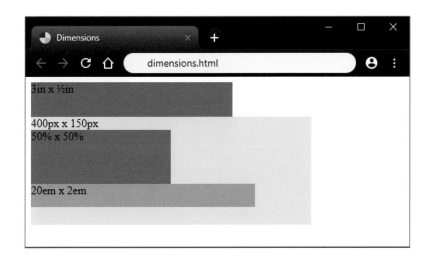

The name of the **em**
unit originates from
typography, where it
represented the width
of the letter "M" in
the current font set.
It is different in CSS
though, as it represents
the height of the
current font. It is often
considered good practice
to use **em** units for text
size wherever possible –
for maximum flexibility.

Control Borders

Each content box can have a border comprising **border-width**, **border-color**, and **border-style** properties. A value can be specified to each of these individual properties to apply a uniform border to all four sides of the content box, or a space-separated list of values can be specified to apply different borders to each side:

- When two values are listed, the first is applied to the top and bottom borders.

- When three values are listed, the first is applied to the top border, the second is applied to the left and right borders, and the third is applied to the bottom border.

- When four values are listed, they are applied clockwise to the top, right, bottom, and left borders.

The default **border-width** value is **medium** (a computed value), and the default **border-color** value is inherited from the element's **color** property, but the default **border-style** is **none**. This means that the border will not be visible until a value is assigned – possible **border-style** values are **solid**, **double**, **dotted**, **dashed**, **groove**, **ridge**, **inset**, **outset**, **hidden**, and **none**.

Rather than creating separate style rules for the **border-width**, **border-color**, and **border-style** properties, it is simpler to use the CSS shorthand technique that specifies a value for each of these three properties to a **border** property as a space-separated list. This uniformly styles each side of the content box with a border of the specified width, color, and style. For example, a style rule declaration of **border : 0.5in dotted Red ;** would apply a half-inch wide red dotted border to all four sides of the content box.

If it is desirable to have different styles, the borders on each side of a content box can be individually styled by creating rules for the element's **border-top**, **border-right**, **border-bottom**, and **border-left** properties. The CSS shorthand technique can also be used with these properties to specify a width, color, and style for the individual side as a space-separated list. For example, a style rule declaration of **border-bottom : 0.5in red dotted** would apply a half-inch wide red dotted border to just the bottom side of the content box.

36

The **outset** border style can be used to create the appearance of a raised button – and the **inset** border style can be used to create the appearance of a depressed button.

1 Create an HTML document containing four paragraphs
```
<p id="no1">Solid - Inherit - Medium</p>
<p id="no2">Top: Dotted - LightSalmon - 0.5em
        <br>Bottom: Dashed - DarkSalmon - 0.5em</p>
<p id="no3">Ridge Double - MistyRose - 1em</p>
<p id="no4">Outset - Tomato - 1em</p>
```

border.html

2 Save the HTML document then create a linked style sheet with rules to add a border that inherits a color
```
p#no1 { color : Tomato ; border : solid ; }
```

3 Next, add rules with shorthand declarations to create a border above and below the content area only
```
p#no2 { border-top : 0.5em dotted LightSalmon ;
        border-bottom : 0.5em dashed DarkSalmon ; }
```

4 Now, add rules creating a border from separate properties
```
p#no3 { border-width : 1em ;
        border-style : ridge double ;
        border-color : MistyRose ; }
```

5 Then, add a rule creating a border on all four sides using the recommended CSS shorthand technique
```
p#no4 { border : 1em outset Tomato ; }
```

6 Save the HTML document then open the web page in a browser to see the borders

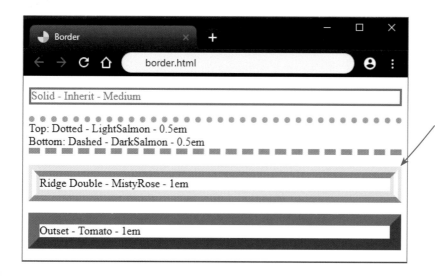

Hot tip

Notice how the browser miters the borders diagonally where they meet – this offers some creative possibilities.

Add Padding

Each content box can have "padding" space added around the core content area by a style rule assigning a value to the **padding** property. A single value can be specified to apply a uniform padding width to all four sides of the content area, or a space-separated list of values can be specified to apply different padding widths to each side:

● When two values are listed, the first is applied to the top and bottom sides and the second is applied to the left and right.

● When three values are listed, the first is applied to the top side, the second is applied to the left and right sides, and the third is applied to the bottom side.

● When four values are listed, they are applied clockwise to the top, right, bottom, and left sides.

The padding area surrounds the core content area and extends to the outer edges of the border area if a border is specified – right up to the beginning of the margin area. The element's background fills the core content area and the padding area, so that any specified background color gets automatically applied to both the core content area and the padding area.

The **padding** property can be specified as a unit value or as a percentage value. When a percentage is specified, the padding width is calculated using the width and height of the containing element – and the padding area size will be adjusted if the size of the containing element gets changed.

Typically, a padding area is specified when adding a border to an element to increase the space between the content and the border.

If it is desirable to have different padding widths on each side of a content box, the padding can be individually styled by creating rules for the element's **padding-top**, **padding-right**, **padding-bottom**, and **padding-left** properties. For example, style rule of **padding-top : 0.5in ; padding-bottom : 0.5in ;** would apply a half-inch padding area to top and bottom sides. Alternatively, the same result can be achieved using the CSS shorthand with a declaration of **padding : 0.5in 0 0.5in 0 ;**.

Beware

Setting padding as a percentage may produce undesirable results when the user resizes the browser window – you can specify unit values to avoid this.

Hot tip

The padding width for each side can always be set using the CSS **padding** shorthand by setting sides requiring no padding to zero – always use the shorthand.

...cont'd

1 Create an HTML document containing three paragraphs that each include a span element and are separated by horizontal ruled lines

```
<p>Horizontally
<span id="pad-h">Padded</span> Content.</p> <hr>
<p>Vertically
<span id="pad-v">Padded</span> Content.</p> <hr>
<p>Horizontally and Vertically
<span id="pad-hv">Padded</span> Content.</p>
```

padding.html

2 Add a style sheet with rules to color the paragraph and span elements

```
p { background : LightSalmon ; }
span { background : MistyRose ;
        border : 0.3em dashed Tomato ; }
```

3 Next, add a style rule to add padding to the left and right sides of the first span content box

```
span#pad-h { padding : 0 3em 0 3em ; }
```

4 Now, add a style rule to add padding to the top and bottom sides of the second span content box

```
span#pad-v { padding : 1em 0 1em 0 ; }
```

5 Then, add a style rule to add uniform padding to all sides of the third span element

```
span#pad-hv { padding : 1em ; }
```

6 Save the HTML document then open the web page in a browser to see the added padding

Notice how the background color fills the content area and padding area – extending right up to the outer edge of the border area.

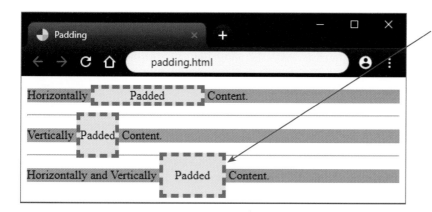

Set Margins

Each content box can have outer transparent "margin" space added around the entire content, padding, and border areas by a style rule assigning a value to the **margin** property. A single value can be specified to apply a uniform margin width to all four sides of the content box, or a space-separated list of values can be specified to apply different margin widths to each side:

- When two values are listed, the first is applied to the top and bottom sides and the second is applied to the left and right.

- When three values are listed, the first is applied to the top side, the second is applied to the left and right sides, and the third is applied to the bottom side.

- When four values are listed, they are applied clockwise to the top, right, bottom, and left sides.

The **margin** property has a default value of zero but in reality the browser applies its own intrinsic default values to allow spacing between elements. For example, heading elements always allow a margin area before a following paragraph element.

The **margin** property can be specified as a unit value, or as a percentage value, or with the **auto** keyword to have the browser compute a suitable margin. When the **auto** keyword is specified to an element's **margin** property, the browser first calculates the distance to the left and right of that element, up to the boundaries of its containing element, then divides the total in half to compute the value of each side margin. For example, applying a **margin : auto ;** rule to a paragraph element of 80px width, that is contained within an outer division element of 400px width, the browser divides the total difference of 320px in half then applies 160px wide margins to each side of the paragraph element – so it gets positioned centrally within the containing division element.

If it is desirable to have different margin widths on each side of a content box, the margin can be individually styled by creating rules for the element's **margin-top**, **margin-right**, **margin-bottom**, and **margin-left** properties. For example, style rule declarations of **margin-top : 0.5in ; margin-bottom : 0.5in ;** would apply a half-inch margin area to top and bottom sides. Alternatively, the same result can be achieved using the CSS shorthand with a declaration of **margin : 0.5in 0 0.5in 0 ;**.

Hot tip

The margin width for each side can always be set using the CSS **margin** shorthand by setting sides requiring no margin to zero – always use the shorthand.

...cont'd

1 Create an HTML document with an outer division element that contains three inner division elements
```
<div class="container"> Centered Block
<div class="zero">Default Position</div>
<div class="center">Centered Block</div>
<div class="offset">Offset Block</div>
</div>
```

margin.html

2 Add a style sheet with rules to center the outer division within the page, and create a border around the division
```
div.container { margin : auto ;
                border : 0.3em dashed Tomato ; }
```

3 Next, add style rules to remove all margins from the first inner division, and to color its background
```
div.zero { margin : 0 ; width : 10em ;
           background : LightSalmon ; }
```

The ability to automatically compute the margin size is essential for centering content.

4 Now, add style rules to center the second inner division, to create a border, and to color its background
```
div.center { margin : auto ; border : 0.3em dashed Tomato ;
             width : 10em ; background : MistyRose ; }
```

5 Then, add style rules to add top and left margins to the third inner division, and to color its background
```
div.offset { margin : 20px 0 0 20px ;
             background : LightSalmon ; }
```

6 Save the HTML document then open the web page in a browser to see the margin styles

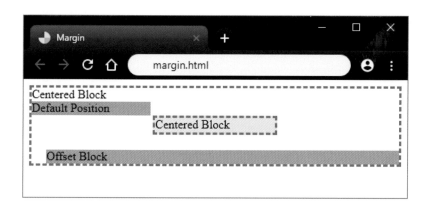

Notice that **margin:auto;** centers the block but not the text within that block. See page 64 for text alignment styles.

Position Boxes

When laying out the element content boxes of a web page, the CSS **position** property has a default value of **static** – representing the normal flow positioning scheme. Assigning a different value to an element's **position** property allows that element's place to move from the normal flow so it can be positioned independently.

Alternatives to the default **static** value can be specified using the **absolute, relative, fixed,** and **sticky** keywords to specify an alternative positioning scheme to that of the normal flow layout.

The **absolute, relative, fixed,** and **sticky** positioning schemes each use one or more of the CSS "offset" properties **top, right, bottom,** and **left,** to define the element's position.

When the position property is specified as **absolute,** the positioning scheme places the element at the specified offset distance from the boundaries of its containing element. For example, an absolutely positioned division element with **top** and **left** values of **100px** will be positioned 100 pixels below and to the right of the boundaries of its containing element.

When the position property is specified as **relative,** the positioning scheme adjusts the position of an element relative to the place it would originally occupy in the normal flow layout. For example, specifying a **top** value of **-18px** moves the selected element up, and specifying a **left** value of **100px** moves it to the right – but crucially, the space occupied by its original layout position is preserved. Applying these relative position values to a span element within a paragraph has this effect:

> a repositioned span element
>
> There is   on this line, but it pays no heed to other
> paragraph content for it is an inline content box.

Notice how the original content is shifted from its normal flow layout position into a newly-created content box positioned at the specified distance relative to its original position. This relative position will be maintained, even when the position of the outer containing element is changed.

So while **absolute** positioning may typically control the position of the outer element, the **relative** positioning scheme is often useful to control the position of nested inner elements.

Don't forget

Absolutely positioned elements and relatively positioned elements move along with the rest of the page when the page gets scrolled.

Beware

Notice how a negative value is used here – these can be used with other properties too but may sometimes produce unexpected results.

1 Create an HTML document with two division elements that each contain a span element
```
<div class="left">
<span>Normal Flow Element</span></div>

<div class="right">
<span class="offset">Relatively Positioned Element
</span></div>
```

position.html

2 Add a style sheet with rules to specify the size of the division elements, and to add borders to all elements
```
div { width : 250px ; height : 100px ; }
div,span { border : 2px solid Tomato ; }
```

3 Next, add style rules to absolutely position the division elements
```
div.left { position : absolute ; top : 20px ; left : 20px ; }
div.right { position : absolute ; top : 80px ; left : 245px ; }
```

4 Now, add style rules to relatively position a span element
```
span.offset { position : relative ; top : 70px ; left : 25px ; }
```

5 Save the HTML document then open the web page in a browser to see the division elements positioned at absolute coordinates on the page, and to see a span positioned relative to the borders of its container

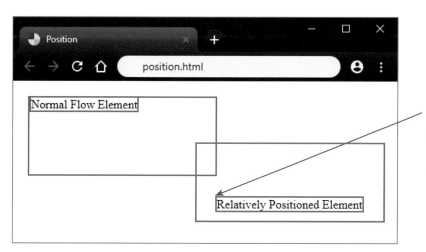

Hot tip

Remember that the position values specify the position of the top-left corner of the target element. Here, it's offset 70 pixels down and 25 pixels to the right.

Fix Positions

A **fixed** positioning scheme, like the **absolute** positioning scheme, completely removes the selected element's content box from the normal flow layout. But unlike **absolute** positioning, where offset values relate to the boundaries of the containing element, in **fixed** positioning the offset values relate to the viewport – the position is relative to the browser window, not to any part of the document.

Usefully, element positions can be fixed to emulate a frame-style interface where some frames remain at a constant position regardless of how the regular page is scrolled. For example, a logo frame could be fixed at a bottom corner of the page so it remains constantly visible even when the page is scrolled.

A **sticky** positioning scheme can also be used to ensure an element remains visible when the user scrolls the page. This initially places an element relative to other elements on the page and maintains this position when the page gets scrolled until it reaches a specified offset position in the viewport. At that point, the element assumes a fixed position and sticks in place. Scrolling back to the specified offset position causes the element to resume its relative positioning.

As with fixed positioning, element positions can be sticky to emulate a frame-style interface. For example, a banner frame could stick at the top of the viewport so it remains constantly visible even when the page is scrolled.

To use the **sticky** positioning scheme you must specify a threshold offset position to at least one of the element's **top**, **bottom**, **left**, or **right** properties, otherwise it will remain relatively positioned when the user scrolls the page.

Beware

At the time of writing, the Safari web browser does not support the **position : sticky ;** rule. You must include a **position : -webkit-sticky ;** rule for that browser until this feature is implemented in Safari.

HTML

fixed.html

1 Create an HTML document containing a heading, two divisions, and a tall image

```
<h1>Fixing Elements</h1>
<div class="sticky">Sticky Banner Element</div>
<div class="fixed">Fixed Logo Element</div>
<img src="ruler.png" alt="Tall Ruler">
```

2 Add a style sheet with rules to specify the size and colors of the division elements

```
div { width : 150px ; padding : 10px ;
        background : Tomato ; color : White ; }
```

3 Next, add style rules to make the first division element stick centered at the top of the page when scrolled
div.sticky { position : **sticky ; top** : **10px ; margin** : **auto ; }**

4 Now, add style rules to fix the second division element at the bottom right of the page when scrolled
div.fixed { position : **fixed ; bottom** : **0px ; right** : **0px ; }**

5 Save the HTML document then open the web page in a browser and scroll the page to see the division elements remain visible

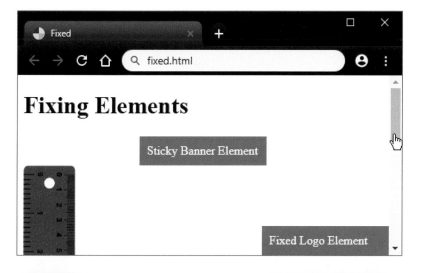

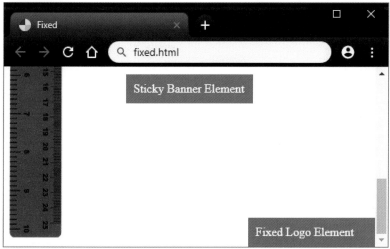

ruler.png – 70px x 525px

Stack Boxes

Changing from the **static** default positioning scheme, by assigning the **absolute** value to the **position** property, allows elements to overlap – stacking one above the other in the same order they are listed in the HTML code.

The stacking order can be explicitly specified, however, in CSS by assigning an integer value to the **z-index** property of each element. The element with the highest value appears uppermost, then beneath that appears the element with the next highest value, and so on.

Hot tip

The value specified to the **z-index** property to determine the stacking order can be either a positive integer, such as **1**, or a negative integer, such as **-1**.

So the **absolute** positioning scheme allows element position to be precisely controlled in three dimensions using XYZ coordinates – along the X axis with the **left** and **right** offset properties, along the Y axis using the **top** and **bottom** offset properties, and along the Z axis using the **z-index** stacking order property.

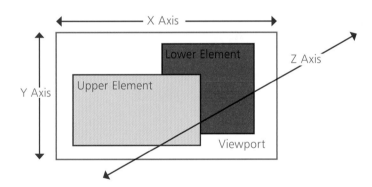

Specifying a value to the **z-index** property of stacked elements allows you to control whether elements should appear in front or behind other elements – regardless of the order in which they are listed in the HTML document.

It is often useful to stack elements containing text above an image element to add text labels to the image.

stack.html

1   Create an HTML document containing three division elements and an image element
```
<div class="container">
<img src="scene.png" alt="Street Scene">
<div class="btm-label">Street Scene</div>
<div class="top=label">Paris, 1966</div>
</div>
```

...cont'd

2 Add a style sheet with rules to position the outer division element at the bottom of a stack

div.container { **position** : absolute ;
top : 0px ; **left** : 0px ; **z-index** : 0 ; **}**

3 Next, add rules to position a division element on the next level in the stack

div.top-label { position : absolute ; **color** : Red ;
top : 10px ; **right** : 20px ; **z-index** : 1 ; **}**

4 Now, add rules to position a division element on the uppermost level in the stack

div.btm-label { position : absolute ; **color** : Red ;
bottom : 10px ; **left** : 220px ; **z-index** : 2 ; **}**

5 Save the HTML document then open the web page in a browser to see the elements positioned in all three dimensions to add text labels above the image

scene.png
500px x 350px

Float Boxes

The CSS **float** property allows a content box to be positioned at the side boundary of its containing element – using the **left** or **right** keywords to specify the preferred side. Typically, this feature is used to flow text around images that have been floated to the side of a containing paragraph element.

You can also explicitly prevent text flowing alongside a floated content box using the CSS **clear** property – specifying **left, right,** or **both** keywords to determine which side must be clear, so that text will begin below the floated content box.

float.html

viper-front.png
150px x 128px

viper-rear.png
155px x 115px

1 Create an HTML document containing three paragraphs and two images
```
<p>Massive acceleration - the forbidden fruit! It's easy to avoid such unlawful
<img src="viper-front.png" alt="Viper Front">
activities in a normal vehicle. But there is an evil serpent; a Viper that tempts you to take a bite out of the asphalt. With a tasty 500-hp V10 powering a mere 3,300-lb roadster, the Dodge Viper SRT-10 tricks you into playing music with the loud pedal.</p>

<p>This car is too excessive, too epic for most people to use on a daily basis.
<img src="viper-rear.png" alt="Viper Rear">
But for otherwise nice couples who need only two seats this is the car that will shame those who come up against them.</p>

<p class="clear">If you can afford to...
                 Buy one. You'll like it.</p>
```

2 Add a style sheet with a rule to color all paragraph backgrounds
```
p { background : LightSalmon ; }
```

3 Next, add style rules to float the first image to the right side of its containing paragraph element and add a border
```
img[src="viper-front.png"] {
        float : right ; border : 2px dashed Tomato ; }
```

4 Now, add style rules to float the second image to the left side of its containing paragraph element and add a border
```
img[src="viper-rear.png"] {
        float : left ; border : 2px dashed Tomato ; }
```

5 Save the HTML document then open the web page in a browser to see the floated images

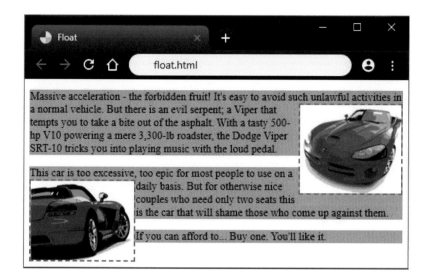

Floated content boxes are not removed from normal flow layout but merely repositioned within it – the space at their original position gets filled with surrounding content.

6 Edit the style sheet to add a rule that prevents the final paragraph flowing alongside the second floated image
p.clear { clear : both ; }

7 Save the HTML document again and refresh the browser to see the final paragraph is now below the second image

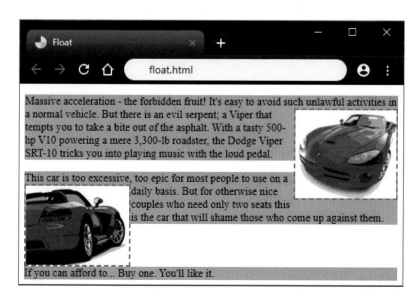

With CSS any element can be floated to the side of its containing element by setting its **float** property.

Handle Overflow

Although CSS provides many controls to specify the precise size and position of content boxes, there is no guarantee that their content will fit neatly within their boundaries in all circumstances. For example, consider the effect of increasing the font size of text content that fits snugly within a block-level content box – the text may then "overflow" outside the box boundaries.

Overflowing content is generally **visible** by default, but the CSS **overflow** property can specify alternative handling behaviors using the **hidden** or **scroll** keywords. With **overflow : hidden ;** the overflowing content will be invisible, but with **overflow : scroll ;** the browser will provide horizontal and vertical scrollbars that the user can use to view the overflowing content.

Beware

The **overflow** property is only effective for block elements that have a specified height, otherwise the block will automatically accommodate the content.

You can control whether the browser provides only a horizontal scrollbar, or only a vertical scrollbar, for the user to view hidden content with **overflow-x** and **overflow-y** properties. These accept a value of **hidden** to hide the individual scrollbar, or a value of **scroll** to provide an individual scrollbar. For example, with the style rule **overflow-x : hidden ;** the horizontal scrollbar is not provided, whereas **overflow-y : scroll ;** provides a vertical scrollbar.

Text content will normally wrap to the next line within a block-level content box at word breaks, as the **whitespace** property is set to **normal** by default. You can, however, disable text wrapping with a **whitespace : nowrap ;** style rule. As overflowing content is generally **visible** by default, the text will then appear on a single line extending beyond the boundary of the content box.

If it is undesirable to display overflowing text, you can hide it with the **overflow : hidden ;** rule as with other content. Additionally, you can specify how overflowing text is treated with a style rule using a **text-overflow** property. This can accept a **clip** value, which truncates the text characters without regard to word breaks, or it can accept an **ellipsis** value, which replaces the final truncated letters with an ... ellipsis – to indicate that text has overflowed.

overflow.html

1 Create an HTML document with six division elements

```
<div class="vis"><img src="berry.png" alt="Berry"></div>
<div class="hid"><img src="berry.png" alt="Berry"></div>
<div class="scr"><img src="berry.png" alt="Berry"></div>
<div class="ver"><img src="berry.png" alt="Berry"></div>
<div class="hor"><img src="berry.png" alt="Berry"></div>
<div class="txt">CSS for Cascading Style Sheets</div>
```

2 Add a style sheet with rules that specify the block type and size of the divisions – as less than the image size
div { display : inline-block ; **width** : 80px ; **height** : 130px ; **border** : 2px dashed Tomato ; **margin-right** : 60px ; **}**

3 Next, add style rules to handle the image overflow
div.vis **{ overflow** : visible ; **}**
div.hid **{ overflow** : hidden ; **}**
div.scr **{ overflow** : scroll ; **}**

4 Now, add style rules to control individual scrollbars
div.ver **{ width** : 120px ;
        overflow-x : hidden ; **overflow-y** : scroll ; **}**
div.hor **{ height** : 150px ;
        overflow-x : scroll ; **overflow-y** : hidden ; **}**

5 Then, add style rules to handle the text overflow
div.txt **{ white-space** : nowrap ;
        overflow : hidden ; **text-overflow** : ellipsis ; **}**

6 Save the HTML document then open the web page in a browser to see how the overflow has been handled

berry.png
100px x 130px

Hot tip

Notice the different treatment of overflow...
Visible
Hidden
Scroll

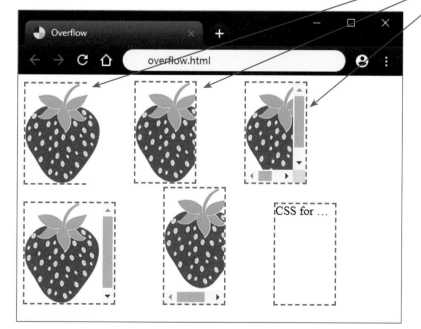

Layout Pages

The arrangement of content boxes on a web page can create many different layouts, but one of the most common layout schemes divides the web page into a header, a navigation bar, side bars, main content, and a footer – as illustrated below.

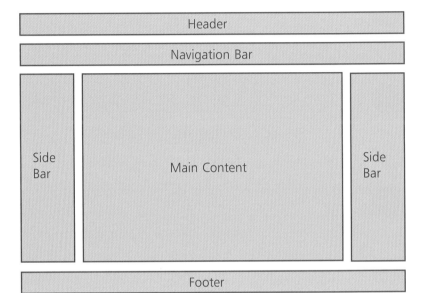

- **Header** – the name of the website and often a logo image
- **Navigation Bar** – hyperlinks to pages of the website
- **Main Content** – the most important part of the web page
- **Side Bars** – supplemental information or advertisements
- **Footer** – details such as copyright and contact information

To best achieve a web page layout it is important to include a universal **margin : 0px ;** style rule to override the browser's default margin size.

You should also include a universal **box-sizing : border-box ;** style rule that allows the content boxes' padding and border to be included within each element's total width and height. This means that borders and padding will not be added outside the size you specify for each element – so you have better control.

Hot tip

You can discover more about the **box-sizing** property on page 124.

1 Create an HTML document with six division elements
```
<div>Header</div>
<div>Navigation Bar</div>
<div class="column side">Side<br>Bar</div>
<div class="column main">Main Content</div>
<div class="column side">Side<br>Bar</div>
<div class="footer">Footer</div>
```

layout.html

2 Add a style sheet with universal overriding rules
```
* { margin : 0px ; box-sizing : border-box ; }
```

3 Next, add style rules to add padding and borders to each division element – now included within their total size
```
div { padding : 5px ; border : 1px solid Tomato ; }
```

4 Now, add rules to size and float three division elements
```
div.column { float : left ; height : 200px ; }
div.side { width : 15% ; }
div.main { width : 70% ; }
```

You can adjust the percentage values of the three column divisions, but added together they must total 100%.

5 Finally, add a style rule to position the final division
```
div.footer { clear : both ; }
```

6 Save the HTML document then open the web page in a browser to see the layout

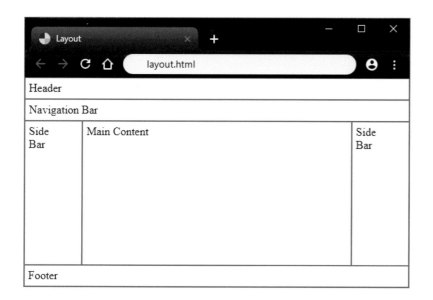

This is the traditional CSS method to create a 3-column layout, but you will discover more modern responsive layout methods later in this book.

Summary

- Content on a web page is displayed within invisible rectangular boxes that are either block-level or inline.

- Block-level content boxes add line breaks before and after the box and have optional areas for **padding, border,** and **margin.**

- Inline content boxes do not add line breaks or support rules for width, height, top/bottom margin, and padding.

- Inline-blocks appear inline but unlike regular inline content boxes they do support rules for **width** and **height.**

- When assigning any non-zero value to a property, the declaration must include a two-letter unit name.

- A **border** can be added around a content box by a rule specifying a width, a color, and a border style.

- A **padding** space can be added around the core content area by a rule specifying a padding size.

- Padding and borders are added outside the core content area that is set by a rule specifying an element's **width** and **height.**

- Transparent **margin** space can be added around the content, **padding,** and **border,** by a rule specifying a margin size.

- Content boxes can be placed on the web page at **absolute, relative,** or **fixed** positions.

- The stacking order of overlapping content boxes can be determined by a rule specifying a **z-index** integer value.

- A content box to be positioned at the side boundary of its containing element by a rule specifying a left or right side.

- Overflowing content is generally visible but can be made invisible by a rule specifying a **hidden** or **scroll** option.

- To best achieve a web page layout it is important to include a universal rule to override the browser's default **margin** size.

- Padding and borders can be included in an element's width and height by a rule specifying **box-sizing** as **border-box.**

3 Manipulate Text Content

Suggest Font

A CSS style rule can suggest a specific font to be used by the browser for the display of text content in a selected element by specifying the font name to its **font-family** property. The browser will use the specified font if it is available on the user's system – otherwise it will display the text using its default font.

The default font may not be the best choice for the author's purpose, so CSS additionally allows the **font-family** property to suggest a generic font family from those in the table below:

Above are serif (left) and sans-serif (right) versions of a letter – the serif decorations are circled. Serif font characters are generally considered to be more readable but sans-serif is better for small font sizes and for text aimed at children.

Font Family:	Description:	Example:
serif	Proportional fonts where characters have different widths to suit their size, and with serif decorations at the end of the character strokes	Times New Roman
sans-serif	Proportional fonts without serif decorations	Arial
monospace	Non-proportional fonts where characters are of fixed width, similar to type-written text	Courier
cursive	Fonts that attempt to emulate human hand-written text	Segoe Script
fantasy	Decorative fonts with highly graphic appearance	Castellar

Hot tip

Develop the habit of enclosing all named fonts within quotes.

The browser will first try to apply the named font, but in the event that it is unavailable will select a font from those available that most closely matches the characteristics of the generic preference. In this way, the appearance of the text should at least approximate the author's intention, even without specific font-matching.

In a style rule **font-family** declaration, the preferred font name should appear before the generic font family preference separated by a comma. Multiple named fonts can be specified as a comma-separated list – all before the generic font family preference. Font names that include spaces must be enclosed within quote marks or they will not be recognized by the browser.

…cont'd

family.html

1 Create an HTML document containing a paragraph with several spanned sections of text

```
<p>The <span class="serif">City of New York</span>
was introduced to professional football on the same day
that the city was introduced to the
<span class="fantasy">New York Giants</span>.
It was a clear sunny
<span class="mono">October afternoon in 1925</span>
when the Giants took the field to play against the
<span class="cursive">Frankford Yellow Jackets</span>.
</p>
```

2 Add a style sheet containing a rule suggesting a default font for the entire paragraph

```
p { font-family : "Arial Narrow", sans-serif ; }
```

3 Next, add style rules suggesting fonts for the spanned text

```
span.serif { font-family : "Times New Roman", serif ; }
span.fantasy { font-family : "Castellar", fantasy ; }
span.mono { font-family : "Courier", monospace ; }
span.cursive { font-family : "Comic Sans", cursive ; }
```

4 Save the HTML document then open the web page in a browser to see the sections of text appear in the named fonts or in a generic family font

It is good practice to specify a generic font family preference in every **font-family** declaration.

Set Size

CSS provides a number of ways to specify the size of text in a style rule declaration by assigning values to the **font-size** property. The most obvious way is as an absolute size using any of the units listed on page 34 – for example, **font-size : 12pt ;**. Additionally, CSS provides a number of keywords to specify a relative size:

Keyword:	Equivalent:
xx-large	24pt
x-large	17pt
large	13.5pt
medium	12pt
small	10.5pt
x-small	7.5pt
xx-small	7pt

Using the keywords listed in the table on the left, the **medium** size is the browser's default font size, and the rest are computed relative to that size.

Where the browser's default font size is **12pt**, the computed values might look something like those listed in the table.

It is preferable to use **em** units or percentage values to specify sizes relative to the browser's default font size. For example, where the browser's default font size is **12pt**, a value of **1em** (or **100%**) is equivalent to a font size of 12 points – so **1.5em** (or **150%**) would be equivalent to a font size of 18 points in that case.

A further refinement is to specify the **font-size** property with values in **vw** ("viewport width") units, where a value of **1vw** is 1% of the current viewport width. This allows the size of text to resize to suit the size of viewing device or browser window.

The thickness or "weight" of text can be easily adjusted using the CSS **font-weight** property and the **bold** and **normal** keywords.

Specifying a **bold** value to a selected element's **font-weight** property causes normally weighted text to appear in a heavier font, and specifying a **normal** value causes heavily weighted text to appear in a lighter font. In reality, the browser uses two different fonts to achieve this effect – for **normal** text it uses a regularly weighted font (for example "Verdana") but it switches to the heavier weighted variant of that font if one is available (such as "Verdana Bold") for **bold** text.

...cont'd

1 Create an HTML document containing four paragraphs
```
<p>Medium sized text at the default size</p>
<p class="lg">Large sized text at 150%</p>
<p class="sm">Small sized sans text at 60%</p>
<p class="huge">Bold text at double size</p>
```

size.html

2 Add a style sheet containing a rule to specify the browser's default font size relative to the viewport
```
body { font-size : 4vw ; }
```

3 Next, add a rule to specify font size for the second paragraph
```
p.lg { font-size : 1.5em ; }
```

4 Now, add rules to specify font size and a generic font family for the third paragraph
```
p.sm { font-size : 0.6em ; font-family : sans-serif ; }
```

Sans-serif fonts are considered to be more readable for smaller text.

5 Finally, add rules to specify font size and font weight for the fourth paragraph
```
p.huge { font-size : 200% ; font-weight : bold ; }
```

6 Save the HTML document then open the web page in a browser to see each paragraph's font size and weight

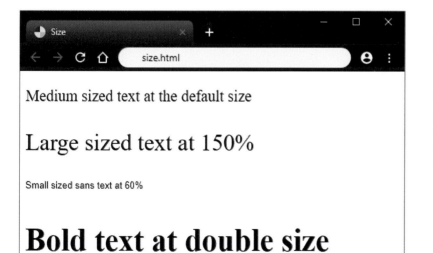

With this example you can resize the browser window to see the font size change to suit the current viewport area.

Vary Style

Slanting text

A CSS **font-style** property can request the browser to use a slanting variant of the current font by specifying the **italic** or **oblique** keywords – these are subtly different.

When the **italic** keyword is specified, the browser seeks an italicized variant of the current font in its font database. This is an actual font set, similar to the current upright font but graphically different to produce slanting versions of each upright character.

When the **oblique** keyword is specified, the browser seeks an oblique variant of the current font in its font database. This may be an actual font set – a slanting version of the current upright font – or alternatively, it may be a generated version in which the browser has computed a slanting version of the upright font. Either may be mapped to the **oblique** keyword in the browser's font database and called upon by the CSS **font-style** property.

In reality, using either **italic** or **oblique** keywords typically produces the same italicized text appearance, and in each case upright text can be resumed by specifying the **normal** keyword to the element's **font-style** property.

Small capitals

A CSS property called **font-variant** can specify a **small-caps** value to allow text characters to be displayed in a popular small capitals format using uppercase characters of two different sizes. Uppercase text in the selected element will appear as large capital characters, but lowercase text will appear as smaller capitals.

The browser may achieve the small capitals effect using a smaller capital from the font set, or by generating a computed smaller version. Once again, regular text can be resumed by specifying the **normal** keyword as the **font-variant**.

Hot tip

You can specify the **small-caps** value to the **font-variant** property of heading elements to make document headings more interesting.

1 Create an HTML document containing four headings
```
<h1>A Heading with Regular Font Style</h1>
<h1 class="ital">A Heading with Italic Font Style</h1>
<h1 class="caps">A Heading with Small Capitals</h1>
<h1 class="caps">A Heading
<span class="norm">with Mixed</span> Variants</h1>
```

HTML

variant.html

2 Add a style sheet containing a rule to specify an italic font style for the second heading
```
h1.ital { font-style : italic ; }
```

3 Next, add a rule to specify a small capitals font variant for the third heading
```
h1.caps { font-variant : small-caps ; }
```

4 Now, add rules to specify that part of the fourth heading should return to normal from a small capitals font variant, and add a background to emphasize the change
```
span.norm { font-variant : normal ;
                background : LightGreen ; }
```

5 Save the HTML document then open the web page in a browser to see each heading's font style and variant

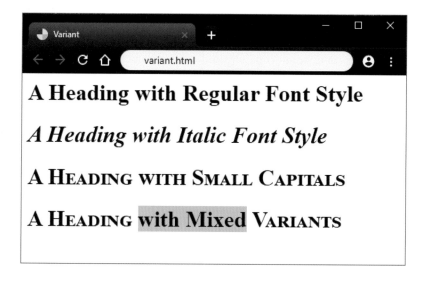

Use Shorthand

Usefully, CSS provides a **font** property to which various font preferences can be specified in a combined single rule stating:

font-style | font-variant | font-weight | font-size | font-family

Appropriate values can be assigned to each part of the combined **font** shorthand property – for example, like this:

p { font : italic small-caps bold medium "Times", serif ; }

The **font-size** and **font-family** values are mandatory, but the first three values for **font-style**, **font-variant**, and **font-weight** properties are optional and may appear in any order. Values for each one of these three optional properties may be completely omitted and a **normal** value will be automatically assumed.

It is important to recognize that values not explicitly specified will still have a **normal** value applied – no value is inherited from the containing element, and this can produce some unexpected results. For example, a style rule selecting a span element within a containing paragraph element styled by the rule above might look like this:

span { font : large cursive ; }

The values explicitly specified in this rule will be applied to the **font-size** and **font-family** properties of the span element, and a **normal** value will be applied to its **font-style, font-variant,** and **font-weight** properties – so text within the span element does not inherit the **italic, small-caps,** or **bold** values from the paragraph.

One further possibility available with a combined **font** rule is the option to specify a **line-height** (the spacing between each line) by adding a forward slash and unit value after the **font-weight** value. This is useful to establish a common standard line spacing where various font sizes appear.

Beware

Remember that a **normal** value is applied for each part of a combined **font** rule unless explicitly specified – and this will override the current parent element value.

font.html

1 Create an HTML document containing a paragraph with several spanned sections of text

```
<p>
<span class="head">The Sneakers Game</span><br>
In 1934 the
<span class="giant">New York Giants</span> beat the
<span class="bears">Chicago Bears</span>, by
<span class="score">30-13</span>,
in nine-degree temperatures [
```

```
<span class="venue">at the Polo Grounds</span>
] in a game that has become famous as the "Sneakers
Game." With the <span class="giant">Giants</span>
trailing <span class="score">10-3</span> at the half,
head coach <span class="coach">Steve Owen</span>
provided his squad with basketball shoes to increase
traction on the icy turf. The team responded with four
touchdowns in the second half to turn the game into a
<span class="giant">Giants</span> rout. </p>
```

2 Add a style sheet with font rules for the paragraph and
for each of the span elements
```
p { font : normal small/1.3em "Courier",monospace ; }
span.head { font : 350% "Pristina", cursive ; }
span.giant { font : small-caps large "Castellar", fantasy ; }
span.bears { font : large "Arial", sans-serif ; }
span.score { font : bold small "Verdana", sans-serif ; }
span.venue { font : italic medium "Arial", sans-serif ; }
span.coach { font : medium "Comic Sans MS", cursive ; }
```

3 Save the HTML document then open the web page in a
browser to see the styles applied using the font shorthand

In 1934 the NEW YORK GIANTS beat the **Chicago Bears,** by **30-13,** in nine-degree temperatures [*at the Polo Grounds*] in a game that has become famous as the "Sneakers Game." With the GIANTS trailing **10-3** at the half, head coach **Steve Owen** provided his squad with basketball shoes to increase traction on the icy turf. The team responded with four touchdowns in the second half to turn the game into a GIANTS rout.

Hot tip

Always use the **font** shorthand property rather than the individual **font-style**, **font-variant**, **font-weight**, **font-size**, and **font-family** properties.

Align Text

English language text in a paragraph is normally horizontally aligned to the left edge of the paragraph, and this is the default behavior to display text in a paragraph element's content box.

Additionally, CSS provides a **text-align** property that can explicitly specify how text should be horizontally aligned within the paragraph element's content box using the keywords **left**, **center**, **right**, or **justify**. As expected, the **left** value aligns each line to the paragraph's left edge, the **right** value aligns each line to the paragraph's left edge, and the **center** value aligns each line centrally between both edges.

Perhaps more interestingly, the **justify** value aligns each full line to both left and right edges of the content box and adjusts the spacing between characters and words to make each line the same length.

In displaying lines of text, the browser automatically computes the line height to suit the content size – typically this will be the height of the font x 1.2. The browser then displays the text vertically centered in invisible "line boxes" of the computed height.

The CSS **vertical-align** property can explicitly specify how text should be vertically aligned using the keywords **baseline**, **sub**, and **super**. The **baseline** value specifies central vertical alignment: the default behavior. The **sub** and **super** values increase the boundaries of the outer container in which the line box exists, and shift the text down or up respectively to display subscript or superscript.

Content can also be shifted up or down by specifying positive or negative unit values, or percentage values, to the **vertical-align** property. Alternatively, the **top**, **middle**, and **bottom** keywords can specify vertical alignment with top-most, middle, or bottom-most content.

Two other keywords of **text-top** and **text-bottom** can be specified to the **vertical-align** property in order to vertically align other inline content boxes, such as those of image elements, to the top or bottom edge of a line box.

The **text-align** property only controls alignment of text within a content box – it is not used to center content boxes. See pages 40-41 for details on how to center content boxes.

Usually subscript and superscript is much smaller than the text – create the vertical shift by specifying **sub** or **super** values then apply a **font** rule to reduce the shifted text's size.

1 Create an HTML document containing three paragraphs
```
<p>Enjoy the sunsets, the restaurants, the fishing, the
diving... the lifestyle of the Florida Keys!</p>
<p class="just">Enjoy the sunsets, the restaurants, the
fishing, the diving... the lifestyle of the Florida Keys!</p>
<p>Line <span class="up">Superscript</span>
<span class="down">Subscript</span>
<span class="top">Top</span></p>
```

align.html

2 Add a style sheet with rules to specify font and colors
```
p, span { font : medium monospace ;
background : LightGreen ; border : 1px solid LimeGreen ; }
```

3 Next, add a rule to horizontally justify the text within the
second paragraph's content box
```
p.just { text-align : justify ; }
```

4 Now, add rules to adjust the vertical alignment of spanned
text within the third paragraph
```
span.up { vertical-align : super ; }
span.down { vertical-align : sub ; }
span.top { vertical-align : top ; }
```

5 Save the HTML document then open the web page in a
browser to see the alignments

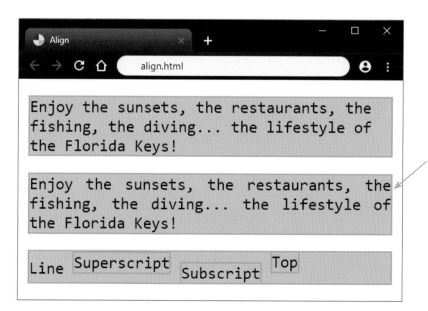

Hot tip

Notice how the **justify** keyword aligns each full line to the edge of the content box and adjusts the spacing between characters and words.

65

Control Space

One of the most common features of printed text is the indentation of the first line of each paragraph to improve readability. This can be easily accomplished for text in HTML paragraphs using the **text-indent** property to specify an indentation size, such as **5em**.

Alternatively, the indentation value may be specified as a percentage where the browser will indent an amount relative to the total line length. For example, given a paragraph element within a division container element of **500px** width, specifying a **text-indent** value of **10%** would indent the start of the first line by **50px** (500 x 10% = 50).

It is also possible to specify negative values for the **text-indent** property, but this can produce inconsistent results so is best avoided.

The amount of space between each word can be adjusted from the **normal** default spacing by explicitly specifying a value to the CSS **word-spacing** property. Note that the specified value is added to the default spacing to increase the space. For example, specifying a unit value of **5em** increases the space to **normal+5em**, not a spacing of **5em** overall.

Similarly, the amount of space between each letter can be adjusted from the **normal** default spacing by explicitly specifying a value to the CSS **letter-spacing** property. This also adds the specified value onto the default spacing to determine the total space. For example, specifying a unit value of **5em** increases the space to **normal+5em**, not a spacing of **5em** overall.

Both **word-spacing** and **letter-spacing** properties accept the **normal** keyword to resume normal spacing. Also, they may both be overridden by the **text-align** property, described on page 64, that has precedence in determining the appearance of the entire line.

Hot tip

The **word-spacing** and **letter-spacing** properties can both accept negative values – to produce some interesting results.

…cont'd

1 Create an HTML document with two paragraphs containing spanned text

```
<p>The Geologic Story at the
<span class="spread">Grand Canyon</span>
attracts the attention of the world for many reasons, but
perhaps its greatest significance lies in the geologic record
preserved and exposed here.</p><p>The rocks at
<span class="spread">Grand Canyon</span>
are not inherently unique but the
<span class="space">variety of rocks clearly exposed
present a complex geologic story.</span> </p>
```

space.html

2 Add a style sheet containing a rule to indent the start of each paragraph

```
p { text-indent : 5em ; }
```

3 Next, add style rules to increase the letter spacing and set a background color on two spanned sections of text

```
span.spread { letter-spacing : 1em ;
              background : LightGreen ; }
```

4 Now, add style rules to increase the word spacing and set a background color on the other spanned text

```
span.space { word-spacing : 1.5em ;
             background : LawnGreen ; }
```

5 Save the HTML document then open the web page in a browser to see the indentations and spacing

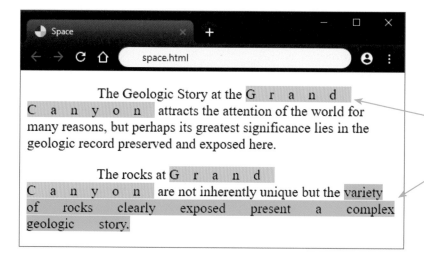

Hot tip

Notice the increased letter spacing and increased word spacing.

67

Decorate Text

Style rules can add decorative lines to text content using the CSS **text-decoration** property with keywords **underline**, **overline**, and **line-through**. These behave as expected adding a line below, a line above, and a line through the text respectively.

Some users may not recognize hyperlinks if their default underline is removed.

Usefully, the CSS **none** keyword can be specified to the **text-decoration** property to prevent unwanted decorations appearing – this is particularly popular for displaying hyperlinks without their usual default underline.

Multiple keywords can be specified to the **text-decoration** property as a space-separated list to apply multiple decorations to the text.

An additional way to enhance text with CSS is available using the **text-transform** property to specify capitalization in the selected element with the keywords **uppercase**, **lowercase**, or **capitalize**.

decor.html

1 Create an HTML document with a paragraph containing spanned text and another paragraph containing hyperlinks, separated by a ruled line

```
<p class="main">You know that it's
<span class="under caps">important</span>
when<br>it is
<span class="under">underlined</span>
<br>and that it's been
<span class="thru caps">canceled</span>
when<br>it has been
<span class = "thru">struck through</span>
<br>but you also must remember to<br>
<span class = "rails upper">read between the lines</span>
<br>
<span class="signature lower"> - MIKE MCGRATH</span>
</p>

<hr>

<p>
<a href="https://ineasysteps.com">Regular link</a> |
<a class="plain" href="https://ineasysteps.com">
        Plain link</a>
</p>
```

2 Add a style sheet with rules to specify fonts and colors

```
p.main { font : medium "Courier", monospace ;
                            background : LightGreen ; }
span.signature { font : 2em "Lucida Handwriting", cursive ;
                            color : Green ; }
```

3 Next, add style rules to decorate spanned text with lines

```
span.under { text-decoration : underline ; }
span.thru { text-decoration : line-through ; }
span.rails { text-decoration : overline underline ; }
```

4 Now, add style rules to transform the case of spanned text

```
span.lower { text-transform : lowercase ; }
span.upper { text-transform : uppercase ; }
span.caps { text-transform : capitalize ; }
```

5 Finally, add a style rule to remove the default underline from a hyperlink

```
a.plain { text-decoration : none ; }
```

6 Save the HTML document then open the web page in a browser to see the text decorations and case transformations

Hot tip

Notice how lowercase has been transformed to uppercase, and how uppercase has been transformed into lowercase.

Change Direction

The default treatment of whitespace within text content is to collapse multiple spaces into a single space, but this can be controlled with the CSS **white-space** property. Specifying the **pre** (preserve) keyword preserves all spaces as they appear in the original text, including any line breaks. Conversely, the automatic wrapping of text in a block can be prevented by specifying the **no-wrap** keyword. Additionally, the **pre-wrap** keyword can be specified to preserve spaces while still allowing text to wrap normally, or the **pre-line** keyword can be specified to collapse multiple spaces while preserving line breaks.

The default left-to-right direction of text lines can be changed to right-to-left by specifying the **rtl** keyword to the CSS **direction** property, and the normal direction resumed with the **ltr** keyword.

Interestingly, when the line direction is changed with the **rtl** keyword, the words appear from right-to-left but the order of English language characters is preserved so that each word still reads correctly left-to-right.

Hot tip

You can discover more about Unicode online at **www.unicode.org** and more on character entities online at **www.w3.org**

This intelligent feature also allows text to be presented in different directions on a single line – for example, to incorporate words in languages that are read right-to-left such as Hebrew and Arabic. The browser examines the Unicode value of each character using a complex Bidirectional algorithm to determine which direction each word should be displayed – those characters from right-to-left languages are automatically displayed in that direction, even if they are written logically from left-to-right in the HTML source code. The automatic Bidirectional algorithm can be turned off, however, by specifying the **bidi-override** keyword to a **unicode-bidi** property.

HTML

direction.html

1 Create an HTML document with a paragraph containing Hebrew character entities and stepped whitespace

```
<p>Hebrew "Congratulations" with mazel tov:
&#1502;&#1494;&#1500;  [mazel]
  + &#1496;&#1493;&#1489;  [tov]
    = &#1502;&#1494;&#1500;  &#1496;&#1493;&#1489;
</p>
```

2 Next, begin a definition list with the same entities

```
<dl>
<dt>LTR Default Direction (lines begin at the LEFT):</dt>
<dd class="ltr">&#1502;&#1494;&#1500; [mazel]
&#1496;&#1493;&#1489; [tov]</dd>
```

...cont'd

3 Now, add two more definitions to complete the list, again featuring the same Hebrew character entities

```
<dt>RTL Custom Direction (lines begin at the RIGHT):</dt>
<dd class="rtl">&#1502;&#1494;&#1500; [mazel]
&#1496;&#1493;&#1489; [tov]</dd>
<dt>LTR Explicit Direction + Bidirectional Override:</dt>
<dd class="bidi-off ltr">No longer reads as mazel tov :
&#1502;&#1494;&#1500; &#1496;&#1493;&#1489;;</dd>
</dl>
```

Beware

Generally, the default treatment of right-to-left language characters achieves the desired effect. In practice, overriding the Unicode Bidirectional algorithm is seldom needed.

4 Add a style sheet with rules to color element backgrounds and preserve whitespace in paragraphs

```
p,dd { background : LightGreen ; }
p { whitespace : pre ; }
```

5 Now, add style rules to set the text directions of each definition in the list

```
dd.ltr { direction : ltr ; }
dd.rtl { direction : rtl ; }
dd.bidi-off { unicode-bidi : bidi-override ; }
```

6 Save the HTML document then open the web page in a browser to see the preserved whitespace and changing directions of the text

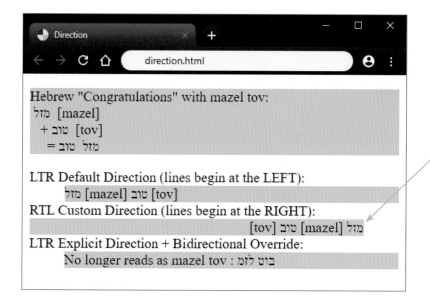

Hot tip

Notice that the **rtl** value displays the characters in the correct order reading from right to left.

Enhance Text

CSS provides five "pseudo-elements" of **::before**, **::after**, **::first-letter**, **::first-line** and **::selection** that can be included in the style rule selector to enhance the content of a selected element.

The **::first-letter** and **::first-line** pseudo-elements are used to add a style to the beginning of text. The **::selection** pseudo element is used to add style to text that has been selected by the user.

The **::before** and **::after** pseudo-elements are used to insert content around the original content. For example, a selector of **p::before** inserts content before the start of each paragraph.

The **::before** and **::after** pseudo-elements specify the content to be inserted to a **content** property in the style rule declaration. Most simply, this can specify a string of text to be inserted. The string must be enclosed in quote marks, but these will not be included in the inserted text – although spaces in the string will be preserved in the inserted text. The **content** property can, however, specify the keywords **open-quote** or **close-quote** to explicitly insert quotes.

Generated content is not limited to text strings, as the CSS **url( )** function can be used to specify non-textual content to the **content** property by stating the path to a resource within the parentheses.

Additionally, the CSS **attr( )** function can be used to specify to the **content** property the name of an attribute within the selected element whose assigned value should be inserted as content.

Multiple items to be inserted can be specified to the **content** property as a space-separated list – using any of the above.

Don't forget

In CSS, all pseudo-elements begin with two colon characters.

pseudo.html

info.pdf

1. Create an HTML document with a heading and four paragraphs that each contain a link to the same resource
\<h1>Pseudo Elements\</h1>

    \<p>Get more \<a href="info.pdf">info\</a> here\</p>

    **\<p>Get more
       \<a href="info.pdf" class="quote">info\</a> here\</p>**

    **\<p>Get more
       \<a href="info.pdf" class="pdf">info\</a> here\</p>**

    **\<p>Get more
       \<a href="info.pdf" class="att">info\</a> here\</p>**

...cont'd

2 Add a style sheet containing rules to style the heading's first letter and selected text – if selected by the user
h1::first-letter { color : Tomato ; }
h1::selection { background : LightSalmon ; }

3 Next, add rules to insert text characters on colored backgrounds before and after the content of each paragraph
p::before { content : "*" ; background : LightGreen ; }**
p::after { content : "!!!" ; background : LawnGreen ; }

4 Now, add rules to insert colored quotes around a link
a[href].quote::before { content : open-quote ; color : Blue ; }
a[href].quote::after { content : close-quote ; color : Blue ; }

5 Then, add a rule to insert an image after a link
a[href].pdf::after { content : url(pdf-ico.png) ; }

6 Finally, add rules to insert a colored attribute value after a link to display the name of the linked resource file
a[href].att::after { content : "(" attr(href) ")" ; color : Blue ; }

pdf-ico.png
32px x 32px

7 Save the HTML document then open the web page in a browser and select part of the heading's text to see the content inserted by CSS style rules

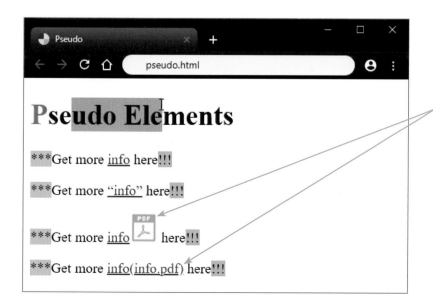

Hot tip

Inserted content is added inside the content box of the selected element – so the enhancements to the links in this example become part of the link.

Number Sections

The CSS ::**before** pseudo-element, introduced in the previous example on pages 72-73, can insert generated content to automatically number sections of an HTML document using the CSS **counter( )** function. This specifies the name of a counter to be inserted into content within its ( ) parentheses.

A counter to count the instances of a selected element must first be created by specifying a chosen name and an incremental value to the **counter-increment** property as a space-separated list.

The counter will begin counting from zero by default and will increment by the specified incremental value for every instance of the selected element. Optionally, the explicitly specified incremental value may be omitted from the rule so the value of 1 will be assumed as the incremental value. For example, a declaration of **counter-increment : num ;** creates a counter named "num" that will start counting from zero and increment by one.

Additionally, the counter can be made to resume counting from a number other than the current count number by specifying the counter name and an integer value from which to count as a space-separated list to the **counter-reset** property. Typically, this will specify a zero integer value to resume counting afresh.

Once a counter has been created it can be inserted before a selected element as generated content by a CSS pseudo-element.

counter.html

1. Create an HTML document with various headings of two different sizes

```
<h2>Topic</h2>
        <h3>Section</h3>
        <h3>Section</h3>
        <h3>Section</h3>

<h2>Topic</h2>
        <h3 class="restart">Section</h3>
        <h3>Section</h3>
        <h3>Section</h3>
```

2. Add a style sheet containing a rule to create a counter for the larger heading elements, which will increment by one

```
h2 { counter-increment : num 1 ; }
```

3 Next, add style rules to create a counter for the smaller heading elements, which will increment by one
h3 { counter-increment : sub 1 ; text-indent : 10% ; }

4 Now, add style rules to insert the current larger heading counter value before each larger heading and set the counter's foreground and background colors
h2::before { content : counter(num) " " ;
                background : Green ; color : White ; }

5 Then, add style rules to insert both the current larger and smaller heading counter value before each smaller heading and set that background color
h3::before { content : counter(num) "." counter(sub) " " ;
                background : LawnGreen ; }

6 Finally, add a style rule to reset the smaller heading counter after each larger heading element
h3.restart { counter-reset : sub 0 ; }

7 Save the HTML document then open the web page in a browser to see the generated counter values inserted before each heading

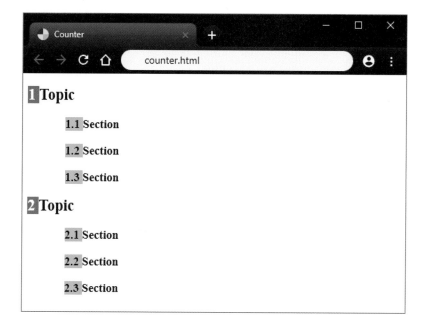

Hot tip

Notice that the generated content in this example includes a space for formatting purposes.

Summary

- Style rules can suggest specific **font** by name and a generic **font-family** as **serif, sans-serif, monospace, cursive,** or **fantasy**.

- A **font-size** can be specified using keywords or absolute sizes, but it is recommended to use relative sizes for flexibility.

- A **font-weight** can be specified as **bold** or **normal**.

- A **font-style** can be specified as **italic** or **normal**.

- A **font-variant** can be specified as **small-caps** or **normal**.

- The **font** shorthand property can be used to specify values for text style, variant, weight, size, and font family.

- The **font-size** and **font-family** values are required when using the **font** shorthand property, but the other values are optional.

- Text can be horizontally aligned within a content box by specifying **text-align** as **left, center, right,** or **justify**.

- Text can be vertically aligned within a content box by specifying **vertical-align** as **top, middle,** or **bottom**.

- The spacing between text can be specified as a unit value to the **text-indent, word-spacing,** and **letter-spacing** properties.

- Text can be decorated by specifying **text-decoration** as **underline, overline,** or **line-through**.

- Text can be transformed by specifying **text-transform** as **uppercase, lowercase,** or **capitalize**.

- Multiple spaces in text are normally collapsed into a single space, but can be preserved using the **white-space** property.

- The default left-to-right direction of text lines can be changed to right-to-left using the **direction** property.

- CSS pseudo-elements can be included after the style rule selector to enhance the content of a selected element.

- Sections of a web page can be automatically numbered using the CSS **counter( )** function.

4 Organize Tables & Lists

Construct Columns

Although web page authors are now discouraged from using HTML tables for page layout, in favor of CSS, tables remain an invaluable format for the presentation of information within the content of a page.

When displaying an HTML table, the browser will, by default, automatically create a table layout sized to accommodate its content. This invariably produces a table with columns of varying width, where each column width is determined by the widest content of any cell in that column. This process requires the browser to examine the table content in some detail before it can compute the optimum table layout and, especially for large tables, can take some time before the browser is able to draw the table.

CSS provides an alternative that allows the browser to quickly compute a suitable table layout without examining the content of the entire table – a fixed layout can be specified to the **table-layout** property of a table element with the **fixed** keyword.

In a **fixed** layout the browser need only consider the **width** value of the table itself and the **width** value of the columns and cells on its first row to determine the table layout, like this:

- The overall table width will be its specified **width** value or the sum of its column **width** values – whichever is the greater.

- A specified column **width** value sets the width for that column.

- When there is no specified column **width** value, a specified cell **width** value sets the width for that column.

- Any columns that have no specified **width** values, for either column or cell, will be sized equally within the table width.

Alternatively, a style rule can explicitly specify that the default table layout scheme should be used, in which the browser computes the column widths according to their content by assigning an **auto** value to the **table-layout** property.

Where tables include a caption element, the position of the caption can be suggested by specifying keywords of **top** or **bottom** to the table element's CSS **caption-side** property.

Hot tip

Specify the first column width and a fixed layout rule to create a first column of custom width and other columns of equal width to each other.

...cont'd

1 Create an HTML document containing two tables with similar content
```
<table><caption>Auto Layout</caption>
<tr><td>Text content</td>
<td>This is text content wider than 130px</td>
<td>Text content</td></tr></table>

<table class="fixed"><caption>Fixed Layout</caption>
<tr><td>Text content</td>
<td>This is text content wider than 130px</td>
<td>Text content</td></tr></table>
```

columns.html

2 Add a style sheet containing rules to specify table width and its features
```
table { width : 500px ; border : 2px dashed DeepPink ;
caption-side : top ; text-align : center ; margin : 0 0 30px ; }
```

3 Next, add style rules to color each table cell and caption
```
td { border : 2px solid DeepPink ; }
caption { background : Pink ; }
```

The **caption-side** property can suggest where a caption might appear but the actual treatment of captions is browser-specific.

4 Now, add a style rule to specify a fixed size column scheme for the second table
```
table.fixed { table-layout : fixed ; }
```

5 Save the HTML document then open the web page in a browser to see tables drawn with both automatic and fixed layout schemes

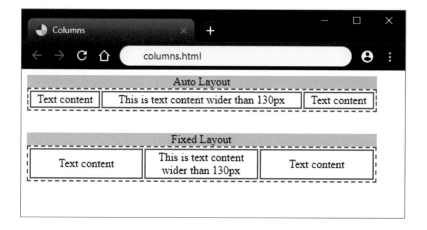

Space Cells

The distance between table cell borders can be specified as a unit value to the CSS **border-spacing** property. This easily allows cells to be spread some distance apart throughout a table.

A single specified **border-spacing** value will be applied uniformly to all cell separations – in much the same way as with the HTML cellspacing attribute.

CSS provides greater flexibility, however, by allowing two values to be specified to the **border-spacing** property as a space-separated list. The first will be applied to the horizontal spacing, at the left and right of each table cell, and the second will be applied to the vertical spacing at the top and bottom of each cell. This means that different distances can be specified for the horizontal and vertical spacing throughout a table.

Another possibility offered by CSS is the ability to hide table cells that contain no content. These frequently occur due to the grid format of tables, which does not always conveniently match the number of cells required – for example, displaying nine content items in a table of five rows and two columns.

Creating a style rule with the CSS **empty-cells** property specifying a **hide** value will cause the browser to not display the border and background of any cell that contains absolutely no content. Cells that contain any content at all, even if it's simply a ** ** (non-breaking space entity), will still be visible.

Conversely, a style rule can explicitly ensure that empty cells are displayed by specifying a **show** value to the **empty-cells** property.

Empty cells that are hidden do continue to have a presence in the table layout inasmuch as their **border-spacing** values are preserved. For example, where the **border-spacing** property is set to **20px**, and the **empty-cells** property specifies a **hide** value, a single empty cell is not displayed, but the surrounding cells remain 40 pixels apart – rather than just a distance of 20 pixels that would exist if the hidden cell did not exist.

Negative values cannot be specified to the **border-spacing** property.

The **empty-cells** property does not apply when a **collapse** value is specified to the **border-collapse** property – see page 82.

1 Create an HTML document containing two tables with similar content – including one empty cell
```
<table>
<tr><td>1</td><td></td><td>3</td></tr>
</table>

<table class="space">
<tr><td>1</td><td></td><td>3</td></tr>
</table>
```

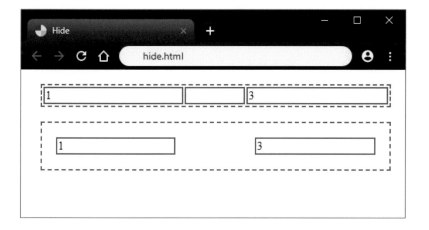

hide.html

2 Add a style sheet containing rules to specify table width and its features
```
table { width : 500px ;
        margin : 20px ; border : 2px dashed DeepPink ; }
```

3 Next, add a style rule to color each table cell and border
```
td { border : 2px solid DeepPink ; }
```

4 Now, add style rules to specify the border spacing and hide empty cells in the second table
```
table.space { border-spacing : 20px ; empty-cells : hide ; }
```

5 Save the HTML document then open the web page in a browser to see tables drawn with both visible and hidden empty cells

Collapse Borders

The borders of adjacent table borders, and table cell borders, can be made to "collapse" into a single border by specifying the **collapse** keyword to the CSS **border-collapse** property. This requires the browser to perform a series of evaluations, comparing the existing borders, to determine how the collapsed border should appear:

- **Visibility Evaluation**: where one of the borders to be collapsed has a **border-style** value of **hidden**, that value takes precedence – so the collapsed border at that location will be hidden.

- **Width Evaluation**: where two visible borders with different **border-width** values are to be collapsed, the highest value takes precedence – so the collapsed border will be the greater width.

- **Style Evaluation**: where two visible borders of equal width are to be collapsed, their **border-style** value sets the precedence in the descending status order of **double, solid, dashed, dotted, ridge, outset, groove, inset** – so the collapsed border at that location will be in the style of highest status. For example, a **double** style wins out over a **solid** style.

- **Color Evaluation**: where two visible borders of equal width and identical style are to be collapsed, the **border-color** value is determined in the descending status order of cell, row, row group, column, column group, table – so that collapsed border will be in the color of highest status. For example, the cell **border-color** wins out over the table **border-color** value.

Don't forget

The **separate** keyword can also be specified to the **border-collapse** property – to explicitly prevent collapsing borders.

The effect of collapsing borders where a table **border-width** of **2px** is compared to a cell **border-width** of **5px** means that the collapsed **border-width** will be 5 pixels – the greater width.

In comparing adjacent **border-style** values of **dotted** and **double**, the collapsed **border-style** will be double – the higher status.

Similarly, comparing adjacent **border-style** values of **dotted** and **solid**, the collapsed **border-style** will be solid – the higher status.

...cont'd

1 Create an HTML document containing two tables with similar content

```
<table><tr>
<td class="twin">1</td>
<td class="dots">2</td>
<td class="full">3</td> </tr></table>

<table class="fold"><tr>
<td class="twin">1</td>
<td class="dots">2</td>
<td class="full">3</td> </tr></table>
```

collapse.html

2 Add a style sheet containing rules to specify table width and its features

```
table { width : 500px ; height : 60px ; margin : 20px ; }
```

3 Next, add style rules to specify the size and color of the table border and each table cell

```
table { border : 2px solid DeepPink ; }
td.twin { border : 5px double DeepPink ; }
td.dots { border : 5px dotted DeepPink ;  }
td.full { border : 5px solid DeepPink ;  }
```

4 Now, add a style rule to collapse the borders of the second table

```
table.fold { border-collapse : collapse ; }
```

5 Save the HTML document then open the web page in a browser to see tables drawn with both regular and collapsed borders

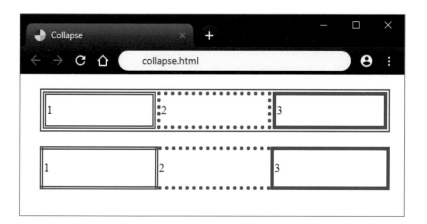

Assign Features

The CSS **display** property can accept a range of values to specify that a selected element should be treated as a table component – emulating the default behavior of HTML tags that a browser automatically applies to table components:

HTML Tag:	CSS Equivalent:
<table>	table
<tr>	table-row
<thead>	table-header-group
<tbody>	table-row-group
<tfoot>	table-footer-group
<col>	table-column
<colgroup>	table-column-group
<th>	} table-cell
<td>	
<caption>	table-caption

The CSS values that can be specified to the **display** property are listed in the table above, together with the HTML tag they most closely represent. These can be used to specify table features to elements of an XML document so a browser will display their content as if it was an HTML table.

xtable.xml

1   Create an XML document that nominates a CSS style sheet to format its element content

```
<?xml version="1.0" encoding="UTF-8"?>
<?xml-stylesheet href="xtable.css" type="text/css"?>
<league><caption>La Liga Top 3</caption>
 <headers>
  <lbl>Position</lbl> <lbl>Team</lbl> <lbl>Points</lbl>
 </headers>
 <rows>
  <team> <pos>1</pos> <name>Barcelona</name>
  <pts>84</pts> </team>
  <team> <pos>2</pos> <name>Real Madrid</name>
  <pts>80</pts> </team>
  <team> <pos>3</pos> <name>Villareal</name>
  <pts>65</pts> </team>
 </rows>
</league>
```

2 Save the XML document then create a style sheet with rules that assign table characteristics to the XML tags
caption { display : table-caption ; }

league { display : table ; }

headers { display : table-header-group ; }

rows { display : table-row-group ; }

team { display : table-row ; }

name, pos, pts, lbl { display : table-cell ; }

xtable.css

3 Next, add style rules that specify the table features
league { margin : auto ; margin-top : 20px ; width : 500px ; border-spacing : 3px ; border : 8px ridge DeepPink ; }

4 Now, add style rules to color the headers and row cells
headers { background : DeepPink ; color : White ; }
rows { background : Pink ; }

5 Save the style sheet alongside the XML document then open the XML document in a browser to see the table

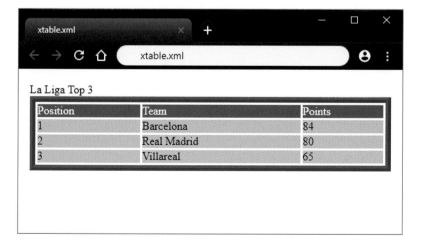

Choose Markers

A list "marker" indicates the beginning of an item in a list – typically a bullet in an unordered **<ul>** list, or an incrementing number in an ordered **<ol>** list. The browser conducts an item count in each case, but usually only uses this to number the items in an ordered list display.

The CSS **list-style-type** property can specify an alternative type of marker for any list – so unordered lists can have numbered markers, and ordered lists can have bullet-points if so desired.

Keywords allow the bullet marker type to be specified as **disc, circle**, or **square**, and number marker types as **lower-roman, upper-roman, decimal**, or **decimal-leading-zero**.

Alphabetical marker types can be specified with the **lower-latin, upper-latin**, and **lower-greek** keywords. Additionally, the CSS specification provides keywords for other alphabets such as **armenian** and **georgian** – but a suitable font is needed for the marker to be displayed correctly by the web browser.

The **list-style-type** property can also specify a **none** value to explicitly suppress the markers so they will not be displayed, although they do remain in the item count.

Optionally, an image may be specified as a marker by stating its path in the parentheses of the CSS **url( )** function to the **list-style-image** property.

markers.html

1 Create an HTML document containing three headings and several ordered lists

```
<h3>Alphabetical list marker types:</h3>
<ol id="list-0"><li>lower-latin<li>...<li>...</ol>
<ol id="list-1"><li>upper-latin<li>...<li>...</ol>
<ol id="list-2"><li>lower-greek<li>...<li>...</ol>

<h3>Bullet list marker types:</h3>
<ol id="list-3"><li>disc<li>...<li>...</ol>
<ol id="list-4"><li>circle<li>...<li>...</ol>
<ol id="list-5"><li>square<li>...<li>...</ol>
<ol id="list-6"><li>image<li>...<li>...</ol>

<h3>Numerical list marker types:</h3>
<ol id="list-7"><li>lower-roman<li>...<li>...</ol>
<ol id="list-8"><li>upper-roman<li>...<li>...</ol>
<ol id="list-9"><li>decimal<li>...<li>...</ol>
<ol id="list-10"><li>decimal-leading-zero<li>...<li>...</ol>
```

...cont'd

2 Add a style sheet with rules to specify heading and list features

```
h3 { clear : left ; margin : 0 ; }
ol {    margin : 0 5px 0 0 ; border : 2px solid DeepPink ;
        float : left ;
        background : Pink ; padding : 0 0 0 10px ; }
li { margin : 0 0 0 20px ; background : White ; }
```

3 Next, add style rules to specify alphabetical list markers

```
ol#list-0 { list-style-type: lower-latin ; }
ol#list-1 { list-style-type: upper-latin ; }
ol#list-2 { list-style-type: lower-greek ; }
```

4 Now, add style rules to specify bullet list markers

```
ol#list-3 { list-style-type: disc ; }
ol#list-4 { list-style-type: circle ; }
ol#list-5 { list-style-type: square ; }
ol#list-6 { list-style-image : url(tick.png) ; }
```

5 Finally, add style rules to specify numerical list markers

```
ol#list-7 { list-style-type: lower-roman ; }
ol#list-8 { list-style-type: upper-roman ; }
ol#list-9 { list-style-type: decimal ; }
ol#list-10 { list-style-type: decimal-leading-zero ; }
```

tick.png – 20px x 20px
Gray areas are transparent.

6 Save the HTML document then open the web page in a browser to see the list markers

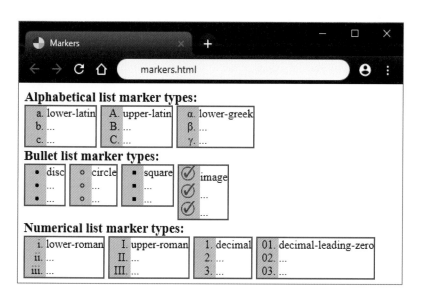

Both numerical and alphabetical markers display the incrementing item count.

Position Markers

Typically, to display a list the browser creates a block-level content box for the entire list and inline content boxes for each list item. Typically, an automatic left margin insets the list item content boxes and each marker appears up against the right edge of this margin area – outside the list item content boxes.

The position of the marker may be explicitly specified to the **list-style-position** property using **inside** or **outside** keywords to determine whether the markers should appear inside the list item content boxes.

Rather than creating separate style rules for the **list-style-type**, **list-style-image**, and **list-style-position** properties, it is simpler to use the CSS shorthand technique that may specify a value for each property as a space-separated list to the **list-style** property. The values may appear in any order, and where any value is omitted, the default value for that property will be assumed.

Lists of either type may be nested with their marker position and type specified independently:

Nested lists can specify they should adopt the **list-style** of the containing element using the **inherit** keyword or suppress markers with the **none** keyword.

list.html

1. Create an HTML document containing three lists plus one nested list

```
<ol class="outside-markers">
 <li>List<li>Markers<li>Outside content box
</ol>

<ol class="inside-markers">
 <li>List<li>Markers<li>Inside content box
</ol>

<ul>
 <li>List<li>Style
 <ol class="inside-markers">
 <li>List<li>Markers<li>Inside content box
 </ol><li>Shorthand
</ul>
```

2. Add a style sheet containing rules to show the list boundaries

```
li { background : Pink ; }
ol,ul { border : 2px solid DeepPink ; }
```

3 Next, add a style rule to specify that some ordered list markers should appear outside the list item content boxes
ol.outside-markers **{ list-style-position : outside ; }**

4 Now, add a style rule to specify that other ordered list markers should appear inside the list item content boxes
ol.inside-markers **{ list-style-position : inside ; }**

5 Finally, add a shorthand style rule that specifies the position, image, and bullet type for the unordered list
ul { list-style : url(star.png) outside square ; }

6 Save the HTML document then open the web page in a browser to see the lists

star.png – 20px x 20px
Gray areas are transparent.

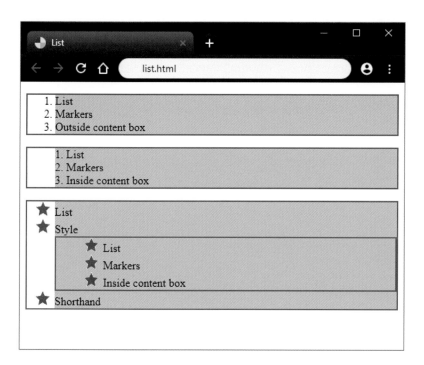

1. List
2. Markers
3. Outside content box

1. List
2. Markers
3. Inside content box

★ List
★ Style
    ★ List
    ★ Markers
    ★ Inside content box
★ Shorthand

Don't forget

The **square** marker type specified by the shorthand rule will be used when the specified image is not available.

Provide Navigation

A navigation bar is simply a list of hyperlinks with particular CSS style rules applied to an HTML list element. Markers are not required, so the **list-style-type** property is specified as **none**, and the browser's default margins and paddings are removed. The hyperlinks in the list are then styled with **display : block ; ,** so that their entire content box is clickable (not just the link text), and **text-decoration : none ; –** to remove the default underlines.

Hyperlinks can indicate status by adding a class for styling, to indicate the current location on the website, and by adding a **:hover** pseudo-class after the selector.

Vertical navigation bars typically specify a fixed **width** value for the list, whereas horizontal navigation bars can instead **float** the list items and hide the **overflow** to maintain visibility of the bar.

navigation.html

1 Create an HTML document containing a list with four hyperlink items
```
<ul>
<li><a href="#home" class="current">Home</a></li>
<li><a href="#info">Information</a></li>
<li><a href="#extra">Extra</a></li>
<li><a href="#contact">Contact</a></li>
</ul>
```

2 Add a style sheet containing rules to remove the markers, margin, and padding, then specify a color and fixed width
```
ul { list-style-type : none ; margin : 0 ; padding : 0 ;
        background : Pink ; width : 150px ; }
```

3 Next, add style rules to display the hyperlinks in blocks and specify how they should appear
```
li a { display : block ; text-align : center ;
        text-decoration : none ;
        color : Black ;  padding : 10px ; }
```

4 Now, add style rules to indicate the hyperlinks' status
```
li a.current { background : HotPink ; }
li a:hover { background : DeepPink ; color : White ; }
```

5 Save the HTML document then open the web page in a browser to see the vertical navigation bar

Hot tip

Pseudo-classes are used to indicate the state of a hyperlink with **a:link** (default), **a:visited**, **a:hover**, and **a:active**.

6 Edit the rules in Step 2 to replace width with overflow
ul { list-style-type : none ; **margin** : 0 ; **padding** : 0 ;
background : Pink ; **overflow** : hidden ; **}**

7 Also edit the rules in Step 3 to add a float rule
li a { display : block ; **text-align** : center ;
text-decoration : none ;
color : Black ; **padding** : 10px ; **float** : left ; **}**

8 Save the HTML document again, then refresh the web
page in your browser to see the horizontal navigation bar

Hot tip

You can discover how
to automatically display
appropriate navigation
for different device sizes
on pages 142-143.

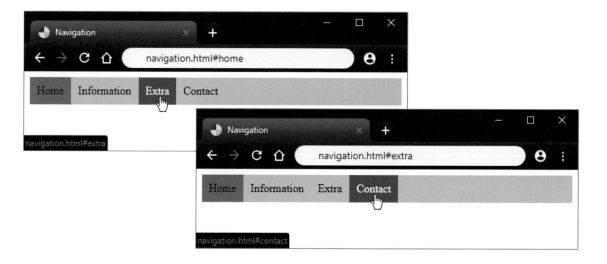

Make Dropdowns

A dropdown box is a content box that is hidden until the user places the cursor over an active element, at which point the box appears to offer further information, a larger image when placing the cursor over a thumbnail image, or a list of clickable options.

The active element should be styled with a **position : relative ;** rule so that the dropdown box can be positioned directly beneath it with a **position : absolute ;** rule. Additionally, the dropdown box should have a specified **z-index** value to place it above any existing content on the page.

It is also useful to include a universal **box-sizing : border-box ;** rule that allows padding and border to be included within the total width and height of the active element and of the dropdown box.

dropdown.html

1 Create an HTML document with a heading, a division element containing two inner divisions, and a paragraph
<h1>Banner</h1>

```
<div class="container">
  <div class="active">Dropdown Menu</div>
  <div class="dropdown">
    <a href="#option-1">Option 1</a>
    <a href="#option-2">Option 2</a>
    <a href="#option-3">Option 3</a>
  </div>
</div>
```

```
<p>Random text content:
        Remains below the dropdown menu.</p>
```

2 Add a style sheet containing a rule to include padding and borders in all elements' total width and height
* { box-sizing : border-box ; }

Hot tip

You can discover more about the **box-sizing** property on page 124.

3 Next, add a rule to create a border around the heading, just to reveal its overall width and height
h1 { border : 2px dashed DeepPink ; }

4 Now, add rules to position the outer division as an inline-block beneath the heading
div.container { position : relative ; display : inline-block ; }

5 Then, add rules to style the first inner division – this will be the active element for the dropdown
div.active { padding : 15px ; background : Pink ; }

6 Next, add rules to position and hide the second inner division – this will be the dropdown content
div.dropdown { position : absolute ; width : 100% ;
border : 2px solid Pink ; background : White ;
z-index : 1 ; display : none ; }

If you do not specify a **background** value for the dropdown content it may be transparent – so the content beneath will remain visible.

7 Now, add rules to make each link's content box clickable
div.dropdown a { display : block ; padding : 15px ;
text-decoration : none ; color : Black ; }

8 Then, add rules to change the link's appearance when the user places the cursor over the link
div.dropdown a:hover { background : DeepPink ;
color : White ; }

9 Finally, add a style rule to reveal the dropdown box when the user places the cursor over the active element
div.container div.dropdown { display : block ; }

10 Save the HTML document then open it and put your cursor over the active element to see the dropdown appear

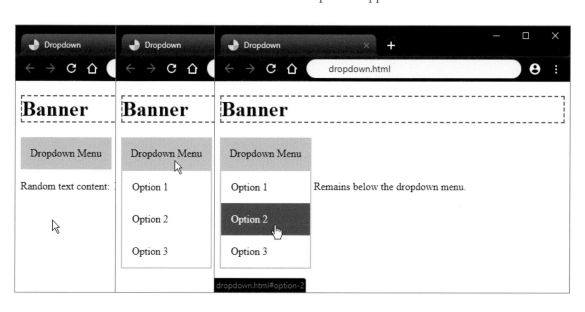

Summary

- A web browser can quickly draw a fixed layout table by assessing the width of the table and its first row of cells.

- A table **caption-side** can be specified as **top** or **bottom**.

- A **border-spacing** can specify the distance between table cell borders as a uniform distance or as horizontal and vertical.

- The **empty-cells** property can hide any cell that contains absolutely no content.

- The **border-collapse** property can combine adjacent borders of a table and its cells into a single border.

- The **display** property can specify that a selected element should be treated by the browser as a table component.

- A **list-style-type** can specify the type of marker to be used for list items as bullets, numbers or letters.

- The CSS **url( )** function can specify the path to an image for use as a list marker.

- A **list-style-position** can specify whether markers should appear inside or outside the list's content box.

- A navigation bar is a list of hyperlinks with particular CSS style rules applied to an HTML list element.

- When a hyperlink is displayed as a **block,** its entire content box is clickable.

- Pseudo-classes can be used to indicate the status of hyperlinks.

- Vertical navigation bars specify a list width, but horizontal navigation bars **float** the list items and hide the **overflow.**

- A dropdown box is a content box that is **hidden** until the user places the cursor over an active element.

- An dropdown's active element should be relatively positioned so the dropdown box can be absolutely positioned beneath it.

5 Generate Effects

Choose Cursors

The CSS **cursor** property can specify the type of cursor to display when the pointer hovers over a selected element. Its default value of **auto** allows the browser to determine which cursor to display, but specifying a **default** keyword will explicitly force the browser to use the operating system's default cursor.

Alternative cursor keywords, together with the cursor icons they represent in the Windows operating system, are listed below:

By default, Windows uses the same resize icon for each diagonal (north-south) but these can be individually different.

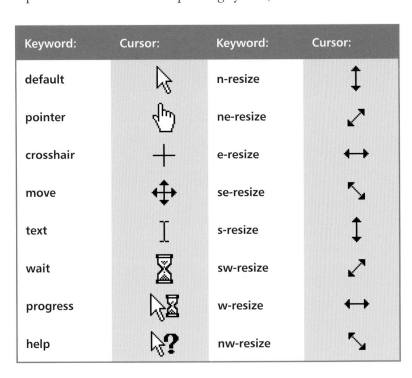

Keyword:	Cursor:	Keyword:	Cursor:
default		n-resize	
pointer		ne-resize	
crosshair		e-resize	
move		se-resize	
text		s-resize	
wait		sw-resize	
progress		w-resize	
help		nw-resize	

The **wait** cursor means that the user should not proceed until the current task has completed, whereas the **progress** cursor allows the user to proceed without delay.

Traditionally, the **pointer** cursor icon indicates a hyperlink, the **move** cursor icon indicates an item that can be dragged, and the **text** cursor icon indicates a component in which text can be selected. As most users are familiar with these cursor conventions, it is best to adhere to them.

In addition to system cursor icons, the **cursor** property can specify an image for use as a custom cursor icon by stating its path within the parentheses of the CSS **url( )** function. Multiple images may be specified, as a comma-separated list, but the list should always end with a regular cursor keyword to specify which system cursor icon to use if the specified images are unavailable.

...cont'd

1 Create an HTML document containing two paragraphs
```
<p class="help-cursor">Browser defined help cursor</p>
<p class="target-cursor">
        Custom cursor (or browser default)</p>
```

cursor.html

2 Add a style sheet with rules to specify border, paragraph height, and color
```
p { border : 2px solid DarkOrange ;
        height : 60px ; background : Bisque ; }
```

3 Next, add style rules to specify cursors for the paragraphs
```
p.help-cursor { cursor : help ; }
p.target-cursor{ cursor : url(target.cur), default ; }
```

4 Save the HTML document then place the pointer over each paragraph to see the cursors

target.cur – 32px x 32px
Gray areas are transparent.

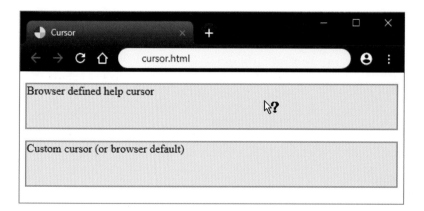

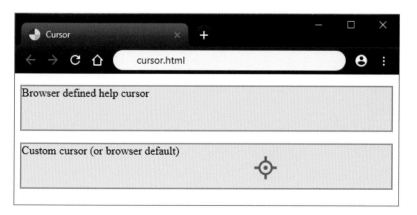

Show Focus

Interactive components of an HTML document comprise those elements that can accept keyboard input, such as a text field, and those that can be activated by a user action, such as a push button or hyperlink. When one of these interactive components is selected by the user, typically by a mouse click or tab key, it is ready to be activated and is said to have "focus".

CSS provides the **:focus** pseudo-class that can be used to apply styling to the element with current focus in a document – in recognition of the user's selection. The styling is removed from that element when the focus shifts to another element, as the user selects a different interactive component.

Indicating the element with current focus is especially useful in lengthy forms with many input fields, as it acts as a marker that easily identifies the progress through the form.

focus.html

1 Create an HTML document containing a form with several interactive components
```
<form action="echo.pl">
<fieldset>
<legend>Send for details</legend>
<label for="addr">Enter your email address: </label>
<input id="addr" type="text"><br>
<input type="submit" value="Send">
<a href = "http://samples">Samples Page</a>
</fieldset>
</form>
```

2 Add a style sheet with a rule to color input elements when in focus
input:focus { background : DarkOrange ; }

3 Next, add a style rule to color hyperlinks when in focus
a:focus { background : Orange ; }

4 Save the HTML document then open the web page in a browser and select each interactive component in turn to see the styles applied

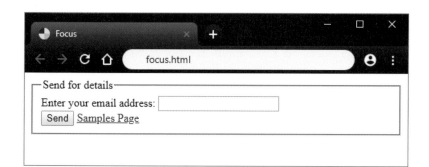

Hot tip

Repeatedly hit the Tab key to move through the interactive components.

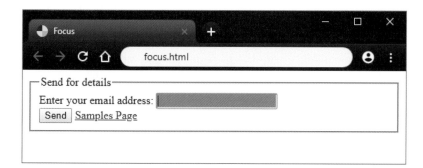

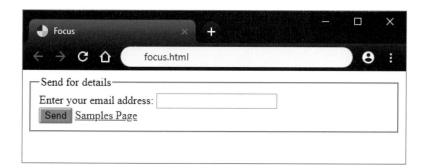

Don't forget

Focus only relates to interactive elements that can receive keyboard input or be somehow activated by the user.

Roll Over

User actions cause interface "events" to which the three dynamic pseudo-classes **:focus**, **:hover**, and **:active** can react. For example, when a user clicks on a text input, the Focus event occurs – to which the **:focus** pseudo-class can react by applying styles. Perhaps more interestingly, when the user moves the cursor onto any element, the MouseOver event occurs – to which the **:hover** pseudo-class can react by applying styles. The applied styles are removed when the cursor moves off the element, as the MouseOut event occurs, creating a dynamic "rollover" effect.

Typically, the rollover will highlight the selected element by changing its content color or background color to become more prominent. A rollover might also specify a different background image to create an image-swap – but this may not work too well on slower connections that need to wait for the new image to download.

A better image-swap alternative is to combine the images for both MouseOver and MouseOut states into a single image file, then have the rollover reveal the appropriate half of the image by specifying a different background position for each state.

prints.png
Gray areas are transparent.

 Create an image file of 150x100 pixels containing top and bottom image areas on a transparent background

rollover.html

2 Next, create an HTML document containing two empty division elements with **id** attributes for style reference
<div id="active"></div> <div id="prints"></div>

3 Add a style sheet with rules to set the divisions' position and size – with height exactly half that of the image
**div { position : absolute ; top : 10px ;
width : 150px ; height : 50px ; }**
div#active { left : 10px ; }
div#prints { left : 170px ; }

4 Next, add style rules to color the backgrounds, and set the background position at the top-left corner of the image, when the cursor is not over the div elements
div#active { background : Bisque ; }
div#prints { background : url(prints.png) 0 0 Bisque ; }

5 Now, add style rules to change the background colors and set the background position at the center-left of the image, when the cursor is over the division elements
div#active:hover { background-color : DarkOrange ; }
div#prints:hover {
        background : url(prints.png) 0 -50px DarkOrange ; }

6 Save the HTML document then open the web page in a browser and roll the cursor over the division elements to see their backgrounds change

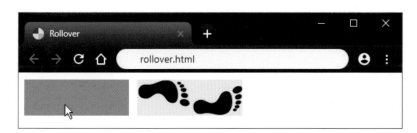

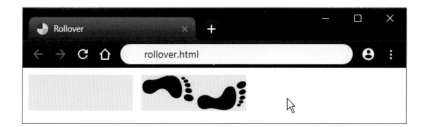

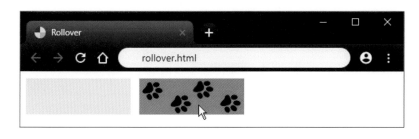

Don't forget

The **:focus** pseudo-class only relates to elements that can receive input – but the **:hover** pseudo-class relates to almost ANY element.

Push Buttons

A rollover effect, as described in the previous example on pages 100-101, can be used with almost any HTML element to create CSS push buttons – for links, scripting, or form submission.

buttons.html
& target.html

echo.pl

1 Create an HTML document with a form that contains three inner elements that will be styled as buttons
```
<a class="button" href="target.html" >Link Button</a>
<button class="button"
        onclick="alert(this.innerText + ' Clicked')">
        Script Button</button>
<form method="GET" action="http://localhost/echo.pl">
<input class="button" type="submit"
        name="CSS" value="Submit Button">
</form>
```

2 Add a style sheet with rules to style each of the three inner elements – removing any default styles
```
.button { display : inline-block ; font : 16px sans-serif ;
        background : Orange ; color : White ;
        border : none ; padding : 16px 32px ; margin : 5px ;
        text-align : center ; text-decoration : none ;
        cursor : pointer ; }
```

3 Next, add rules to create a rollover effect on each button and to simply align the form
```
.button:link, .button:visited { color : White ; }
.button:hover { background : Coral ; }
.button:active { background : OrangeRed ; }
form { display : inline-block ; }
```

4 Save the HTML document then open it in a browser to see the rollover effect on each button

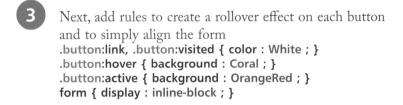

Hot tip

Notice how the selector only specifies the class in this example, to apply the same style rules to various types of element.

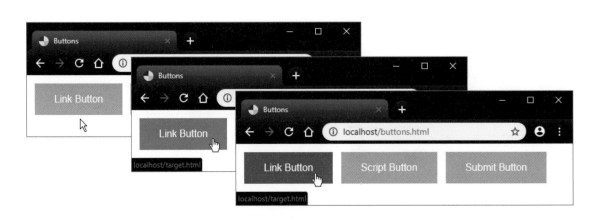

...cont'd

5 Click the link button to open its target page, then return to the buttons page

The target page here contains a single link button that is styled with the same rules as the other buttons.

6 Click the script button to execute the snippet of code assigned to its **onclick** attribute, then close the dialog box

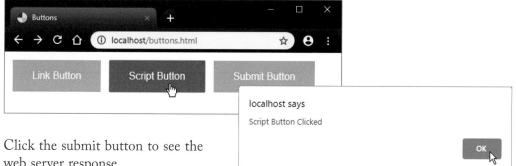

7 Click the submit button to see the web server response

This example is run on a local web server that supports the PERL script **echo.pl** – which processes the form submission and provides the response to the web browser using an external style sheet **echo.css**, and images **abyss.png**, **perl.png**.

Reveal Elements

A dropdown box can be used to reveal larger versions of thumbnail images and, optionally, additional descriptive text. This technique is similar to that used to display the dropdown menu on page 92, so the thumbnail element should be styled with a **position : relative ;** rule so that the dropdown box can be positioned directly beneath it with a **position : absolute ;** rule. Additionally, the dropdown box should have a specified **z-index** value to place it above any existing content on the page.

reveal.html

html.png
& css.png
& js.png – all
330px x 464px

If you do not specify a **background** value for the dropdown content it may be transparent – so the content beneath will remain visible.

1 Create an HTML document with a division that contains a thumbnail image, plus an inner division containing a larger version of the image and some descriptive text
```
<div class="thumbnail">
<img src="html.png" alt="logo" width="35" height="50">
<div class="dropdown">
<img src="html.png" alt="logo" width="135" height="190">
<span class="label">HyperText Markup Language</span>
</div>
```

2 Next, copy and paste the elements in Step 1, then in the copies replace both image sources with **css.png** and replace the descriptive text with **Cascading Style Sheets**

3 Once again, copy and paste the elements in Step 1, then in these copies replace both image sources with **js.png** and replace the descriptive text with **JavaScript**

4 Add a style sheet with rules to position the thumbnail – this will be the active element for the dropdown
```
div.thumbnail { position : relative ; display : inline-block ; }
```

5 Next, add rules to position and hide the second inner division – this will be the dropdown content
```
div.dropdown { position : absolute ; padding : 2px ;
               border : 2px dashed DarkOrange ;
               background : White ;
               z-index : 1 ; display : none ; }
```

6 Now, add a rule to reveal the dropdown content when the user places the cursor over the thumbnail
```
div.thumbnail:hover div.dropdown { display : block ; }
```

7. Finally, add rules to style the descriptive text

```
span.label { display : block ; padding : 15px ;
        text-align : center ;
        background : DarkOrange ; color : White ; }
```

8. Save the HTML document then place the cursor over each thumbnail to reveal the dropdown content

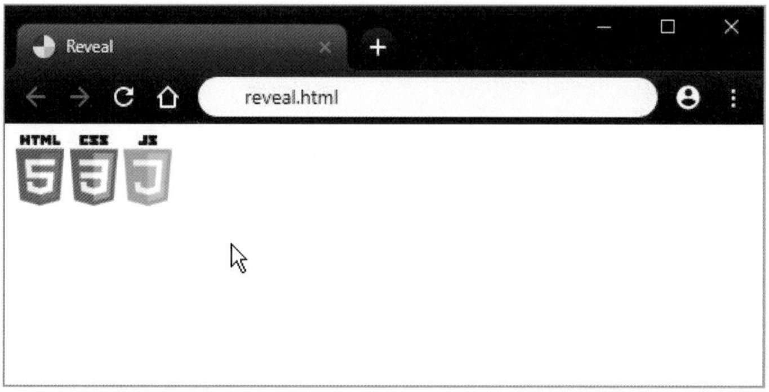

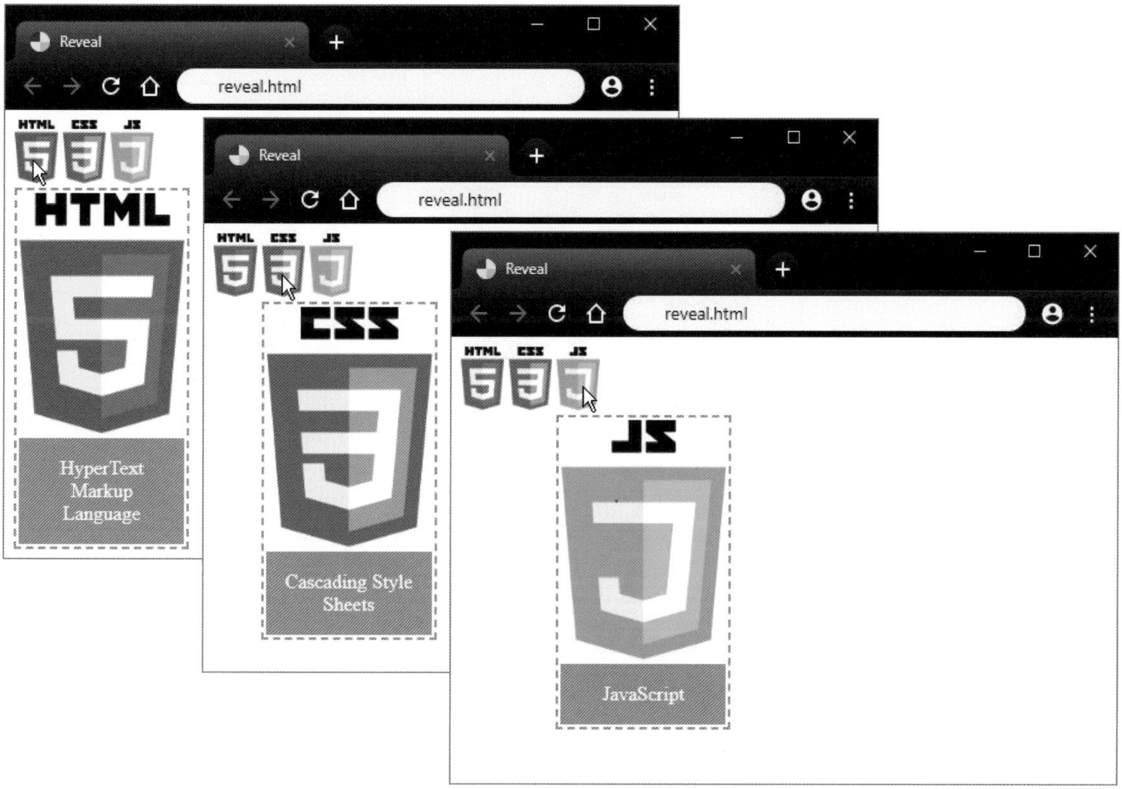

Hot tip

Alternatively, elements can be hidden with a **visibility : hidden ;** rule and revealed with a **visibility : visible ;** rule. With these, the content still occupies space on the page even when hidden, whereas with a **display : none ;** rule, the content is totally removed from the page flow layout.

Draw Corners

The appearance of content box borders can be enhanced by rounding their corners with the CSS **border-radius** property. Where all corners are to have the same radius, this property can specify the radius size as a distance from the corner point in both horizontal and vertical directions – for example, as a value of **20px**.

Individual corners may also be rounded by specifying a radius size to **border-top-left**, **border-top-right**, **border-bottom-right**, and **border-bottom-left** properties.

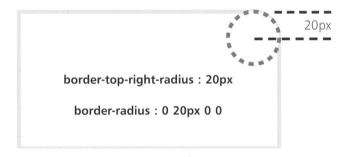

You can create an ellipsis by setting **border-radius** to 50% on an oblong content box.

Alternatively, individual corners may be rounded by using **border-radius** as a shorthand property to specify four values – one value for each corner in the order **border-top-left**, **border-top-right**, **border-bottom-right**, **border-bottom-left**. Where a zero value is specified for any corner, no radius will be produced. Individual corners may also be curved by specifying two values to define an ellipse so the horizontal and vertical directions get a different radius. The first value specifies the horizontal x radius and the second value specifies the vertical y radius. For example, **border-top-right-radius : 20px 50px** defines an ellipse.

Circles can be created by setting the **border-radius** property to exactly half the size (including borders) of a square content box.

1 Create an HTML document with three outer divisions, which each contain one inner division element
**<div class="outer all"><div class="inner">
All Rounded Corners</div></div>**

**<div class="outer ind"><div class="inner">
Individual Corners</div></div>**

**<div class="outer cir"><div class="inner">
Circle</div></div>**

radius.html

2 Next, add a style sheet with rules to specify the position and appearance of each element
div.outer, div.inner { width : 120px ; height : 120px ; }

**div.outer { display : inline-block ; margin : 10px ;
    border : 5px solid DarkOrange ; background : Bisque ; }**

**div.inner { display : table-cell ; text-align : center ;
    vertical-align : middle ; border : 2px dashed Orange ; }**

Notice here how the **table-cell** display style allows the text to be centered horizontally and vertically.

3 Now, add rules to adjust the corners of the outer divisions
div.all { border-radius : 40px ; }

div.ind { border-radius : 50px 0 50px 0 ; }

div.cir { border-radius : 65px ; }

107

4 Save the HTML document then open it in a browser to see the rounded corners

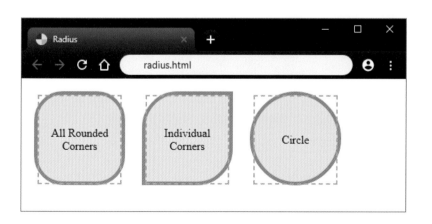

The second outer division in this example could alternatively be styled with individual rules **border-top-left-radius : 50px ; border-bottom-right-radius : 50px ;**.

Cast Shadows

The appearance of content boxes can be enhanced by adding drop-shadow effects with the **box-shadow** property, and text can be similarly enhanced with the **text-shadow** property.

Horizontal and vertical offset values must be specified to position the shadow. Where these are positive values, the shadow will be positioned to the right and below the item. Conversely, negative values can be specified to position the shadow to the left and above respectively – for example, positive values of **20px 10px**.

20px

10px

Optionally, the **box-shadow** and **text-shadow** properties can have a third value to specify a blur distance that determines how blurred the shadow's edge will be – the higher the value, the more blurred. For example, a blur value of **20px** expands the shadow to blur its edge in an area that is 10 pixels either side of the original offset.

Beware

Although specifying a color is not strictly required, it is recommended to avoid inconsistencies between web browsers.

Additionally, a fourth optional value can specify a spread distance, to determine how far the shadow should extend beyond the offset, and the **inset** keyword can be used to create an inner shadow.

You can also add multiple shadows to text by specifying a comma-separated list of shadow values to the **text-shadow** property.

...cont'd

1 Create an HTML document with three outer divisions, which each contain one inner division element

```
<div class="outer drop">
        <div class="inner">HTML</div></div>
<div class="outer glow">
        <div class="inner">CSS</div></div>
<div class="outer inset">
        <div class="inner">JS</div></div>
```

shadow.html

2 Next, add a style sheet with rules to specify the position and appearance of each element

```
div.outer, div.inner { width : 120px ; height : 120px ; }
div.outer { display : inline-block ; margin : 20px ;
  border : 2px solid Black ; background : White ; }
div.inner { display : table-cell ; text-align : center ;
  vertical-align : middle ; font : bold 2em sans-serif ; }
```

3 Now, add rules to apply shadows to boxes and text

```
div.drop { box-shadow : 10px 10px 10px DarkOrange ; }
div.drop > div.inner { text-shadow : 2px 2px DarkOrange ; }

div.glow { box-shadow : 0 0 10px 10px DarkOrange ; }
div.glow > div.inner { color : White ;
                text-shadow : 2px 2px 4px Black ; }

div.inset { box-shadow : 10px 10px 30px DarkOrange inset ; }
div.inset > div.inner { color : Bisque ; text-shadow :
-1px 0 Black , 0 1px Black , 1px 0 Black , 0 -1px Black ; }
```

4 Save the HTML document then open it in a browser to see the shadows

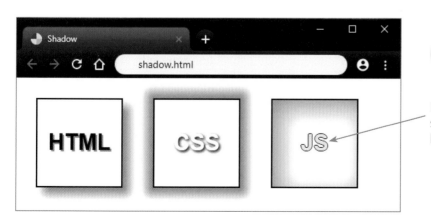

Hot tip

Notice how the multiple shadow rules create a border around the text.

Blend Gradients

CSS provides four functions to create gradient fills, which the browser blends smoothly from one specified color to another – **linear-gradient( )**, **repeating-linear-gradient( )**, **radial-gradient( )** and **repeating-radial-gradient( )**.

The **linear-gradient( )** function creates the color transition along a linear path blending from one "color stop" point to another. Each color stop may be specified in the function's parentheses simply as comma-separated color values, or as comma-separated color and position value – for example, as **Red, Yellow** or as **Red 50%, Yellow 100%** to define color stops at the path's mid-point and end. There must be at least two color stops, but you can specify multiple color stops for more elaborate gradient effects that employ more colors.

The default direction of the **linear-gradient( )** function's path is top-to-bottom, but you can define a different direction by including an optional first value as a combination of keywords **to top bottom left right** – for example, for a diagonal gradient starting at the top left with **to bottom right** keywords. For more precise control of the direction, the optional first value may be specified as an angle, such as **45deg** or **90deg**. In this case, the value specifies the angle between a horizontal edge and **linear-gradient( )** path. For example, **45deg** creates a diagonal path from the bottom left corner to the top right corner, and **90deg** produces a horizontal path from left to right. You can also specify negative values. For example, **-90deg** creates a horizontal path from right to left (as does **270deg**).

The **radial-gradient( )** function also blends from one color stop to another, but the path spreads out from a center point. By default, it begins at the center of the element and is circular. Optionally, the **ellipse** keyword can be specified along with length and position values to define a different radial shape and different center point. You can define a different center point by including an optional first value as a combination of keywords **closest-side**, **farthest-side**, **closest-corner**, **farthest-corner**, **at** and percentage values for the x-axis and y-axis – for example, for a radial gradient starting to the right and below center with **closest-side at 60% 60%**.

The **repeating-linear-gradient( )** and **repeating-radial-gradient( )** functions accept the same values as their non-repeating counterparts, but automatically repeat the gradient after the final specified color stop has been reached.

Each gradient must have at least two color stops.

...cont'd

1 Create an HTML document with four division elements
```
<div class="linear"></div>
<div class="linear-repeat"></div>
<div class="radial"></div>
<div class="radial-repeat"></div>
```

gradient.html

2 Next, add a style sheet with rules to specify the position and appearance of each element – including a default background color
```
div { display : inline-block ; width : 100px ; height : 100px ;
        margin : 10px ; border : 2px solid Black ;
        background : Orange ; }
```

Some browsers may not support gradients so it's useful to specify a default single color.

3 Now, add rules to apply gradient backgrounds for browsers that support gradients
```
div.linear { background :
        linear-gradient( 45deg , DarkOrange, Bisque ) ; }

div.linear-repeat { background :
        repeating-linear-gradient( DarkOrange 20%,
                Bisque 40%, OrangeRed 50% ) ; }
div.radial { background :
        radial-gradient( DarkOrange 20%,
                Bisque 40%, OrangeRed 50% ) ; }

div.radial-repeat { background :
        repeating-radial-gradient( DarkOrange 20%,
                Bisque 40%, OrangeRed 50% ) ; }
```

4 Save the HTML document then open it in a browser to see the gradients

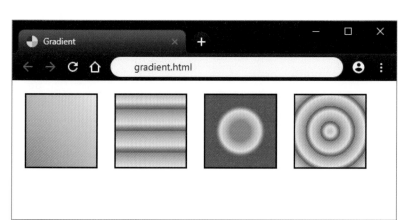

You can specify the same color for the first and last color stops in a repeating gradient to avoid abrupt changes.

Decorate Borders

CSS provides a **border-image** property that allows you to specify an image source to the CSS **url( )** function for decoration of borders. This is the only required value and will position the image within a specified border area, at each corner of a content box.

The **border-image** property can specify additional values, after the image source, to decorate the border areas between the corners – but this works in an unusual manner.

The **border-image** property slices the image into nine sections, like those of a tic-tac-toe board. The first additional value can specify at which points to slice the image from the top, right, bottom, and left edges. For example, a **33%** value will slice one third from each edge. The four corner slices are then placed at each corner of the border, and the four middle slices are then stretched, by default, to decorate the border areas between the corners.

A second additional value can explicitly specify how to decorate the border areas between the corners using these keywords:

- **stretch** – the middle slices stretch to fill the areas (the default).

- **repeat** – the middle slices tile to fill the areas, dividing if necessary.

- **round** – the middle slices tile to fill the areas, rescaling if necessary to avoid dividing.

The **border-image** property is a shorthand property for individual **border-image-source**, **border-image-slice**, and **border-image-repeat** properties. There are also further additional values that can be specified for **border-image-width**, to specify the widths of the border image, and **border-image-outset**, to specify how far the image can extend outside the border area.

All browsers that support the **border-image** property also support gradients. This means that, besides images, you can specify any type of gradient to decorate a border.

1 Create an HTML document with four division elements
```
<div class="image"></div>
<div class="round"></div>
<div class="stretch"></div>
<div class="gradient"></div>
```

decorate.html

2 Next, add a style sheet with rules to specify the position and appearance of each element – including a border
```
div { display : inline-block ; width : 175px ; height : 100px ;
      margin : 10px ; border : 30px solid transparent ;
      background : Bisque ; }
```

3 Now, add rules to decorate the border of each division
```
div.image { border-image : url( stars.png) ; }
div.round { border-image : url( stars.png) 33% round ; }
div.stretch { border-image : url( stars.png) 33% stretch ; }
div.gradient { border-image : repeating-linear-gradient
             ( 45deg, OrangeRed, Orange 20% ) 33% ; }
```

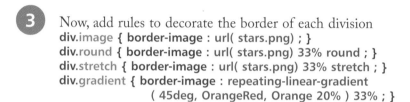

stars.png – 90px x 90px
Gray areas are transparent.

4 Save the HTML document then open it in a browser to see the decorated borders

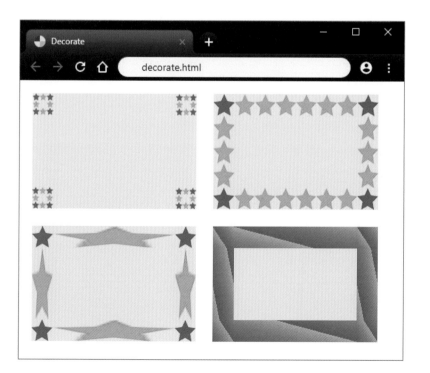

Transform Shapes

CSS can dynamically manipulate content boxes to change their size, position or orientation by specifying one of the transformation functions below to their **transform** property.

You can also specify just one single value to the **scale( )** function to be applied to both the X axis and Y axis.

Function:	Transform:
scale(n1,n2)	Scales X and Y axis all by the ratio *n1 n2*
scaleX(n)	Scales X axis by the ratio *n*
scaleY(n)	Scales Y axis by the ratio *n*
skew(n1,n2)	Scales X and Y axis all by the angle *n1 n2*
skewX(n)	Scales X axis by the angle *n*
skewY(n)	Scales Y axis by the angle *n*
rotate(n)	Rotates by the angle *n* amount
rotateX(n)	Rotates X axis by the angle *n* amount
rotateY(n)	Rotates Y axis by the angle *n* amount
rotateZ(n)	Rotates Z axis by the angle *n* amount
translate(n1,n2)	Moves X and Y axis by *n1 n2* amount
translateX(n)	Moves X axis by n amount
translateY(n)	Moves Y axis by *n* amount
matrix(n,n,n,n,n,n)	Scales by *n, n*, skews by *n, n* translates by *n, n*

The **transform-origin** property can only be used in conjunction with the **transform** property.

The **matrix( )** function is seldom used but it allows you to rotate, scale, move, and skew elements all at once. Its six values, in (somewhat confusing) order, represent the individual functions **scaleX( )**, **skewY( )**, **skewX( )**, **scaleY( )**, **translateX( )**, **translateY( )**.

A "transform origin" is the point around which a transformation is performed and is, by default, the center of the element. You can, however, specify an alternative to a **transform-origin** property as units, percentage values, or keywords **top, bottom, left, right**, and **center**. For example, with **rotate( )** and **transform-origin : top left ;** the element will pivot around its top-left corner, instead of its center point.

Transformations can be specified to the element's **:hover** pseudo-class so the transformation will be performed when the user places the cursor over the element, and will resume its normal state when the user moves the cursor off the element.

...cont'd

1 Create an HTML document with three division elements
```
<div class="rotate">Rotate</div>
<div class="scale">Scale</div>
<div class="skew">Skew</div>
```

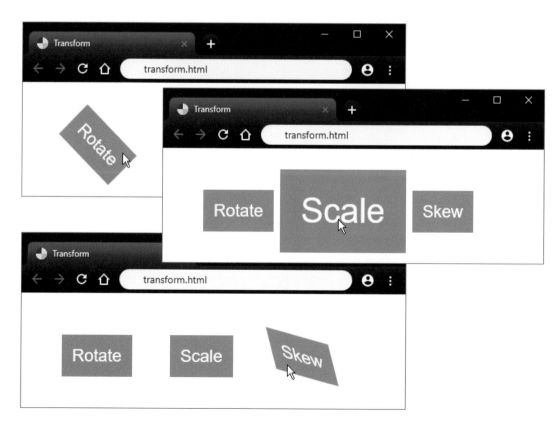

transform.html

2 Next, add a style sheet with rules to specify the position and appearance of each element
```
div { display : inline-block ; margin : 50px 0 0 50px ;
        padding : 15px ; background : DarkOrange ;
        color : White ; font : 1.5em sans-serif ; }
```

3 Now, add rules to transform each division when the user places the cursor over the content box
```
div.rotate:hover { transform : rotate( 45deg ) ; }
div.scale:hover { transform : scale(  2.0, 2.0 ) ; }
div.skew:hover { transform : skew( 15deg, 15deg ) ; }
```

4 Save the HTML document then open it in a browser and place the cursor over each element to see transformations

Make Transitions

CSS can dynamically modify property values to change their color, size, position, orientation, etc. over a specified period of time to create simple animated effects with the **transition** property.

The **transition** property must specify the CSS property that is to be modified, and the duration of the effect – for example, a style rule **transition : width 5s ;** to modify the width of an element over a period of five seconds. Multiple properties can be specified as a comma-separated list of property and duration pairs, such as **transition : width 5s, height 3s ;** to modify both width and height.

You can control the "acceleration curve" of the effect by assigning one of the functions below to a **transition-timing-function** property.

Function:	Transition:
linear	Consistent speed from start to end
ease	Increases from start to reach full speed then decreases at end (default)
ease-in	Increases at start only
ease-out	Decreases at end only
ease-in-out	Increases at start and decreases at end
steps(*n*)	Jump to *n* number of intervals
cubic-bezier(*x1,y1,x2,y2*)	Elastic or bounce between coordinates

Additionally, you can specify a **transition-delay** time value, such as **1s** for one second, so the effect will not begin immediately.

The **transition** property is a shorthand property for individual **transition-property**, **transition-duration**, **transition-timing-function**, and **transition-delay** properties. Values for these may be specified to each individual property or values for all four may be specified, in this order, to the shorthand property – for example, to modify a width, over five seconds, at a consistent speed, after a half second delay with **transition : width 5s linear 0.5s ;**. You can also specify multiple transitions in a comma-separated list of grouped values.

The final value of the property to be modified can be specified to an element's **:hover** pseudo-class – so the transformation will be performed when the user places the cursor over the element.

Don't forget

A transition will not run unless you specify a duration period.

Hot tip

The **steps( )** function jumps to pauses in the transition, so that **steps(5)** pauses each second in a five second effect.

...cont'd

1 Create an HTML document with one division element
`<div class="expand">Transition</div>`

transition.html

2 Next, add a style sheet with rules to specify the position and appearance of the element
```
div { margin : 50px ; padding : 15px ;
         color : White ; font : 1.5em sans-serif ;
         background : Orange ;
         width : 100px ; height : 30px ; }
```

3 Now, add a rule to modify the background, width, and height properties in a five-second transition effect
```
div.expand { transition : background 5s linear 0.5s ,
              width 5s ease-out 0.5s ,
              height 5s steps(5) 0.5s ; }
```

4 Then, add rules to specify the final values of the background, width, and height at the end of the effect
```
div.expand:hover { background : OrangeRed ;
                    width : 350px ; height : 100px ; }
```

5 Save the HTML document then open it in a browser and place the cursor over the element to see the transition

The element will resume its original values when the user moves the cursor off the active element – automatically running the transition effect in reverse.

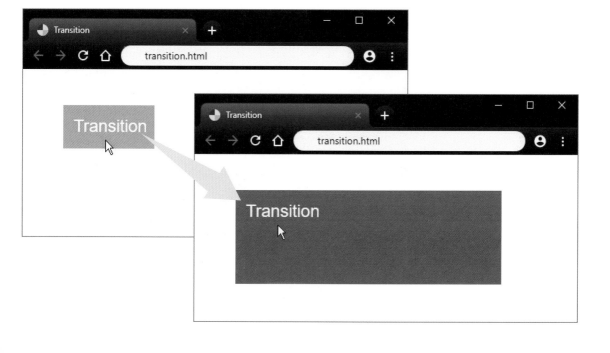

Animate Elements

CSS can dynamically modify property values over a specified period of time with the **transition** property, as described on page 116, but can also nominate "keyframes" to determine property values at particular points for the **animation** property.

Keyframes are created by a CSS **@keyframes** ("at keyframes") rule that defines an animation name and selects points using percentages or **from** (0%) and **to** (100%) keywords – for example, naming an animation "bounce" and selecting three points, like this:

```
@keyframes bounce {
                          from    { top : 100px ; }
                          50%     { top : 150px ; }
                          to      { top : 300px ; }
}
```

Keyframes determine what styles one or more properties will have at various points during an animation.

The **animation** property can specify, in this order, the animation name (defined by the **@keyframes** rule), duration, timing function, delay, iteration count, and direction.

Duration and delay are specified as with transitions, where a value of **5s** represents a period of five seconds.

Timing functions that control the acceleration curve are the same as those for transitions, such as **ease-in-out**, and the iteration count may be an integer or the keyword **infinite**.

Interestingly, the direction can be specified as **normal** (the default), **reverse**, or **alternate** – alternating between playing forward and reverse on successive iterations.

The **animation** property is a shorthand property for individual **animation-name**, **animation-duration**, **animation-timing-function**, **animation-delay**, **animation-iteration-count**, **animation-direction** properties. Values for these may be specified to each individual property or values for all six may be specified, in this order, to the shorthand property – for example, to bind a keyframe named "bounce" to a five-second animation, at a consistent speed, after a one-second delay, to repeat infinitely, in alternating directions, with **animation : bounce 5s linear 1s infinite alternate ;**.

An **animation-fill-mode** can also be added for animations that run for a set number of iterations. This can specify **forwards**, so that the element will retain the values of the final keyframe, **backwards**, so it will get the style values of the first keyframe, or **both**.

Hot tip

You can combine transitions and animations to create some great effects.

...cont'd

1 Create an HTML document with one division element that contains an inner division element
```
<div class="ball">
<div class="label">Animation</div></div>
```

animation.html

2 Next, add a style sheet with rules to specify the position and appearance of the outer division element
```
div.ball { position : absolute ; top : 10px ; width : 120px ;
height : 120px ; color : White ; font : 1.5em sans-serif ;
background : Orange ; border-radius : 50% ; }
```

3 Now, add rules to specify the appearance of the inner division element
```
div.label { display : table-cell ; width : 120px ;
height : 120px ; text-align : center ; vertical-align : middle ; }
```

4 Then, add a keyframe rule to define an animation name and specify points for the animation
```
@keyframes bounce { from { top : 10px ; }
50% { top : 40px ; }
to { top : 100px ; background : OrangeRed ; } }
```

Hot tip

No animation delay is required in this example, so its value is omitted from the style rule and the browser uses its zero default delay value.

5 Finally, add a rule to bind the animation to the outer division element
```
div.ball { animation : bounce 2s linear infinite alternate ; }
```

6 Save the HTML document then open it in a browser to see the animation

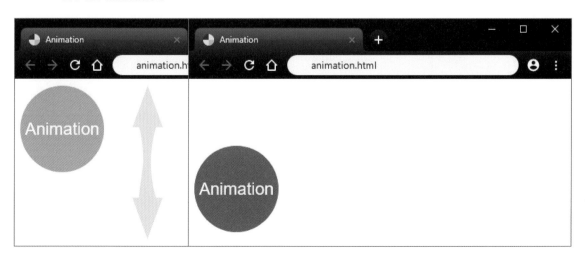

Fit Objects

CSS provides a number of ways in which you can manipulate image or video content. These can be centered within a container simply by making the **<img>** or **<video>** element into a block and setting its left and right margins to the **auto** value.

More interestingly, you can specify how image or video content fits into the **<img>** or **<video>** element itself, using a CSS **object-fit** property. This can determine whether the content should be stretched, squeezed, scaled, or clipped by specifying any of the values listed below:

Value:	Fit:
fill	Content is stretched or squeezed to fill the element's content box (the default)
contain	Content is scaled up or down to maintain its aspect ratio and fit inside the element's content box
cover	Content is scaled to maintain its aspect ratio and fill the element's content box, so may be clipped
scale-down	Content is scaled down to maintain its aspect ratio in smaller content boxes
none	Content is not resized, so may be clipped

Probably the best way to understand how these values affect how the object fits into its content box is by comparison:

fit.html

run.png
150px x 120px

 1 Create an HTML document with six elements that will display the same image – but fit differently
<img src="run.png" alt="Run">

<img class="scale-down short" src="run.png" alt="Run">

<img class="none short" src="run.png" alt="Run">

<img class="fill tall" src="run.png" alt="Run">

<img class="contain tall" src="run.png" alt="Run">

<img class="cover tall" src="run.png" alt="Run">

2 Add a style sheet with rules to specify the appearance and set the width of each element to match the image width
img { display : inline-block ; **border** : 2px solid DarkOrange ;
margin : 5px ; **width** : 150px ; **}**

3 Next, add style rules to set some content boxes shorter, and some taller, than the image height of 120 pixels
img.short **{ height** : 80px ; **}**
img.tall **{ height** : 200px ; **}**

4 Now, add rules to specify how the images should fit their respective content boxes
img.scale-down **{ object-fit** : scale-down ; **}**
img.none **{ object-fit** : none ; **}**
img.fill **{ object-fit** : fill ; **}**
img.contain **{ object-fit** : contain ; **}**
img.cover **{ object-fit** : cover ; **}**

5 Save the HTML document then open it in a browser to compare how the objects fit within each content box

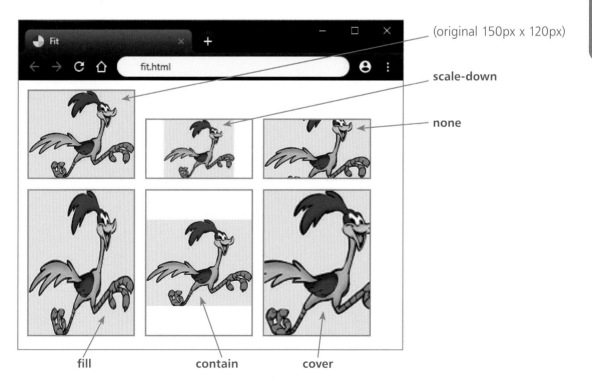

(original 150px x 120px)

scale-down

fill   contain   cover

Summary

- The type of **cursor** icon to display when the pointer hovers over a selected element can be specified using a keyword.

- A currently-selected interactive component of a page can be indicated by specifying a value to the CSS **:focus** pseudo-class.

- Interface events caused by user actions are recognized by the CSS **:focus**, **:hover**, and **:active** pseudo-classes.

- The MouseOver and MouseOut states can be used to create rollover effects for links, scripting, or form submission buttons.

- A relatively positioned thumbnail element can reveal a larger element that is absolutely positioned directly beneath it.

- Content box borders can have rounded corners by specifying a radius size to the **border-radius** property.

- Content boxes and text can have shadows by specifying offset values to the **box-shadow** or **text-shadow** property.

- Linear and radial gradients fill content boxes with colors blended between specified color stop points.

- Content box borders can be decorated by stretching or tiling a sliced image specified to the **border-image** property.

- Transformations manipulate content boxes to change their size, position or orientation.

- Transitions modify property values over a specified period of time to create simple animated effects.

- Animations modify property values over a period of time and nominate keyframes to specify values at particular points.

- Images and videos can be stretched, squeezed, scaled or clipped to fit inside a content box.

6

Control the Web Page

Change Models

Web browsers apply default element styles, contained in their "user agent style sheet", that apply margins and padding values automatically to some elements. For example, the **<body>** element typically gets an 8-pixel margin by default. You can inspect this in most browsers by hitting the F12 key, to open a Developer Tools window, and selecting the body element:

default.html

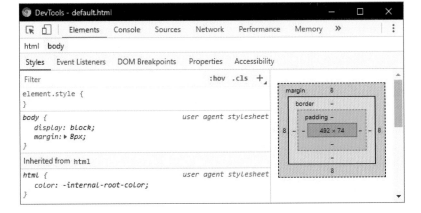

The default value for the CSS **box-sizing** property is **content-box**.

Additionally, the browser's default box model will apply your specified padding and borders outside your specified element size, so the overall size of the element becomes larger than your specification. For example, an **<ul>** list element specified to have a 2-pixel border and a size of 100 x 70 pixels typically gains a 16-pixel margin top and bottom, 40-pixel left padding (for the list markers), and the 2-pixel border outside the content box. This makes the overall size of the element 144 x 106 pixels:

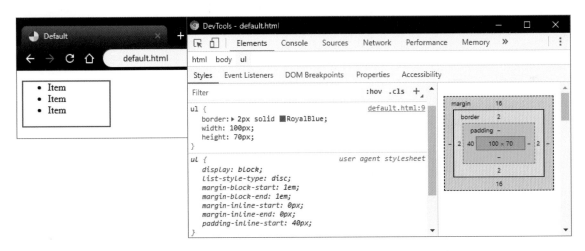

…cont'd

In order to gain control of these default browser behaviors, you can begin each one of your style sheets with these universal rules:

* { margin : 0 ; padding : 0 ; box-sizing : border-box ; }

This overrides the browser's default styles so margins and padding values are no longer automatically applied to elements:

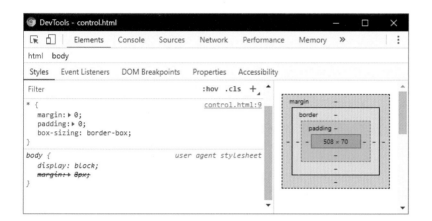

control.html

Additionally, the browser's default box model will no longer apply your specified padding and borders outside your specified element size, so the overall size of the element is exactly as you specified. For example, an **<ul>** list element specified to have a 2-pixel border and a size of 100 x 70 pixels, now gains no margins or padding, and the 2-pixel border is now inside the content box. This makes the overall size of the element 100 x 70 pixels, as intended by your specification:

Hot tip

You now have control and could add a left padding for the list markers if required.

Draw Outlines

CSS provides three properties that can be applied to the user interface, complementing the regular box model. The first two of these can be used to add outlines around an element. The **outline** property accepts the same values that can be specified to the **border** property – for example, **outline : 2px solid RoyalBlue ;** to draw a 2-pixel blue outline around an element.

Crucially, unlike a border, an outline is not part of the element's dimensions, so an element's total width and height is unaffected by the addition of an outline. An outline is drawn on a different level of the Z axis, so may overlap other content.

Additionally, you can add space between an outline and the edge, (or border) of an element by specifying a distance value to an **outline-offset** property – for example, **outline-offset : 5px ;** to add a 5-pixel space between the edge of an element and an outline.

The third property that can be applied to the user interface can be used to allow the user to resize an element, typically by dragging its bottom-right corner. The **resize** property can allow the user to resize an element's size both horizontally and vertically when it specifies a **both** value.

If the user resizes an element to reduce its dimensions, the contents may well overflow, so when using the **resize** property it should be accompanied by an **overflow** style rule to handle the content overflow. It is important that the overflow should be specified as **scroll**, **auto**, or **hidden**, because the **resize** property will not be applied to inline or block elements whose overflow is set to a **visible** value.

Where you want to restrict the user's ability to resize an element in both directions, you can specify a **horizontal** value to the **resize** property – so that the user can only adjust the width of an element by dragging its corner.

Conversely, you can specify a **vertical** value to the **resize** property – so that the user can only adjust the height of an element by dragging its corner.

Don't forget

Setting all elements' **box-sizing** property to **border-box** means that the edge of the element is the same as the edge of any border it has.

...cont'd

1 Create an HTML document containing a division element
`<div class="outline resize">This division has a blue outline and can be resized by dragging its bottom-right corner.</div>`

outline.html

2 Add a style sheet with rules to control the web page
`* { margin : 0 ; padding : 0 ; box-sizing : border-box ; }`

3 Next, add rules to specify the appearance of the division
`div { width : 420px ; margin : 20px ; padding : 10px ;`
`border : 2px solid Black ; background : LightSteelBlue ;`
`font : 1.25em sans-serif ; }`

4 Now, add rules to surround the division with an outline
`div.outline {      outline : 10px solid RoyalBlue ;`
`outline-offset : 5px ; }`

5 Then, add a rule to make the division resizable
`div.resize { resize : both ; overflow : auto ; }`

6 Save the HTML document, then open it in a web browser to see the outline and resize the element

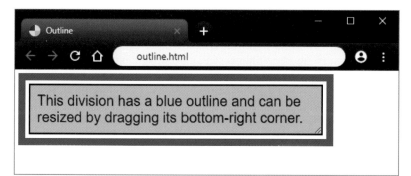

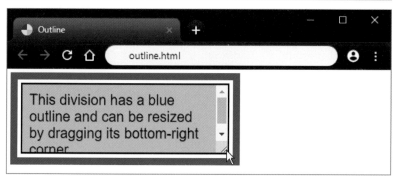

Outlines can overlap page contents.

127

Use Columns

CSS provides a number of properties that make it simple to create multiple-column layouts for text – like those in newspapers.

First, you need to specify an integer value to a **column-count** property to determine the number of columns you want the text divided into – for example, **column-count : 3 ;** for three columns. Typically, this will create a gap ("gutter") between each column that is **1em** wide by default – equivalent to the height of the font. You can also choose your own gutter size by specifying a distance to a **column-gap** property – for example, **column-gap : 50px ;** to create a gap of 50-pixels width between the columns.

With a wider gutter, you can then add a vertical ruled line by specifying width, style, and color values to a **column-rule** property. This accepts the same values as the **border** property, so that a rule of **column-rule : 5px solid RoyalBlue ;** would add blue lines. The **column-rule** property is a shorthand property for individual **column-rule-width**, **column-rule-style**, and **column-rule-color** properties. It must at least specify a style to display a vertical ruled line using default initial values for width and color.

multicol.html

1 Create an HTML document with a division element that contains one heading and some text content
<div class="newspaper">

<h1>The CSS Reporter</h1>
Cascading Style Sheets (CSS) is a style sheet language used for describing the presentation of a document written in a markup language. Although most often used to set the visual style of web pages and user interfaces written in HTML and XHTML, the language can be applied to any XML document, including plain XML, SVG and XUL, and is applicable to rendering in speech, or on other media.

</div>

2 Add a style sheet with rules to control the web page
* { margin : 0 ; padding : 0 ; box-sizing : border-box ; }

3 Next, add rules to add a margin to the division and to specify the appearance of a two-column layout
div.newspaper { margin : 15px ;
                column-count : 2 ;
                column-gap : 50px ;
                column-rule : solid ; }

4 Save the HTML document, then open it in a web browser to see the multiple-column layout

The CSS Reporter

Cascading Style Sheets (CSS) is a style sheet language used for describing the presentation of a document written in a markup language. Although most often used to set the visual style of web pages and user interfaces written in HTML and XHTML, the language can be applied to any XML document, including plain XML, SVG and XUL, and is applicable to rendering in speech, or on other media.

Hot tip

The default **column-rule-color** value here is derived from the text color – adding a color rule for the text will also change the vertical line color to match – for example, **color : Red ;** to change text and line.

5 Edit the rules in Step 3 – to change the appearance to a three-column layout with dotted gutter lines

```
div.newspaper { margin : 15px ;
              column-count : 3 ;
              column-gap : 50px ;
              column-rule : 5px dotted RoyalBlue ; }
```

6 Save the HTML document again, then refresh the web browser to see the new multiple-column layout

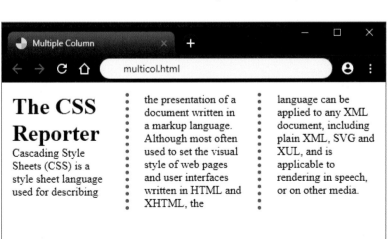

The CSS Reporter

Cascading Style Sheets (CSS) is a style sheet language used for describing the presentation of a document written in a markup language. Although most often used to set the visual style of web pages and user interfaces written in HTML and XHTML, the language can be applied to any XML document, including plain XML, SVG and XUL, and is applicable to rendering in speech, or on other media.

Beware

Setting this example to have many columns will cause the heading to overlap other content – a solution is demonstrated in the example overleaf.

Span Columns

In addition to the **column-count**, **column-gap**, and **column-rule** properties introduced in the previous example on pages 129-129, CSS provides three further properties for use in column layouts.

Where you prefer elements such as headings to span across columns, you can specify how many columns to span as an integer value, or using the keyword **all**, to a **column-span** property.

You can also state a preferred width for the columns by specifying a size to a **column-width** property – but the browser only treats the specified value as a minimum width suggestion. If it cannot fit at least two columns at the specified width, it will revert to a single-column layout.

Lastly, there is a shorthand **columns** property that can be used to specify both **column-width** and **column-count** values. Using both the **columns** and **column-rule** shorthand properties lets you specify a large number of column layout values very concisely.

spancol.html

1 Create an HTML document with a division that contains text content and two headings
`<div class="newspaper">`

`<h1>Professional Word Documents</h1>`
To make your document look professionally produced, Word provides header, footer, cover page, and text box designs that complement each other. You can add a matching cover page, header, and sidebar. Click Insert and then choose the elements you want from the different galleries.

`<h2>Coordinated Document Styles</h2>`
Themes and styles also help keep your document coordinated. When you click Design and choose a new Theme, the pictures, charts, and SmartArt graphics change to match your new theme. When you apply styles, your headings change to match the new theme.

`</div>`

2 Add a style sheet with rules to control the web page
`* { margin : 0 ; padding : 0 ; box-sizing : border-box ; }`

3 Next, add rules to add left and right margins to the division and to specify the appearance of a three column layout –with a suggested column width of 100 pixels

div.newspaper {
        margin : 0 15px ;
        column-gap : 50px ;
        column-rule : 5px solid LightSteelBlue ;
        columns : 100px 3 ; }

4 Now, add rules to specify the appearance of the headings and to have both headings span across all columns

h1, h2 {
        padding : 10px 10px 10px ;
        margin : 20px 0 0 ;
        background : LightSteelBlue ;
        column-span : all ; }

5 Save the HTML document, then open it in a web browser to see the multiple column layout and headings that span across the columns

The **column-rule** property is shorthand for **column-width**, **column-style** and **column-color** properties.

131

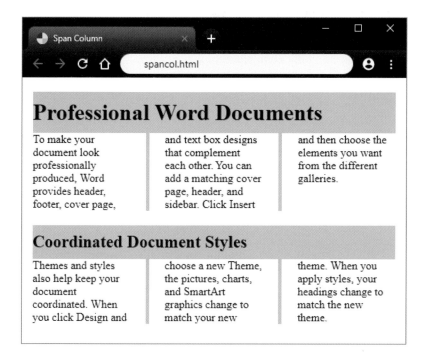

Use Flexbox

Previous examples in this book have displayed content using absolute or relative positioning, and by floating content. These are important, but not ideally suited to create a flexible layout that will respond to various browser screen sizes. To answer this need, CSS introduced the flexible box ("flexbox") layout scheme.

To create a flexible box you must first define an element to be a "flex container" by specifying a **flex** value to its **display** property.

Any inner elements ("flex items") within a flex container will appear on a single row. If the length of the row exceeds the width of the browser, the row will not, by default, wrap onto the next row – unless you specify a **wrap** value to a **flex-wrap** property.

You can also reverse the order of the flex items in the row by specifying a **wrap-reverse** value to the **flex-wrap** property.

So, to create a flexible box that will wrap items onto rows, you will need to specify values to both **display** and **flex-wrap** properties.

Hot tip

Refer back to the absolute and relative positioning example on pages 42-43, and the float layout on pages 52-53.

flexbox.html

Hot tip

All modern browsers support flexbox since:

 Chrome 29.0

 Edge 11.0

 Firefox 22.0

 Safari 10

 Opera 48

1 Create an HTML document with a division element that contains five inner divisions
```
<div class="flex-container">
        <div>One</div>
        <div>Two</div>
        <div>Three</div>
        <div>Four</div>
        <div>Five</div>
</div>
```

2 Add a style sheet with rules to control the web page
```
* { margin : 0 ; padding : 0 ; box-sizing : border-box ; }
```

3 Next, add rules to make the outer division flexible
```
div.flex-container {    display : flex ;
                        flex-wrap : wrap ;
                        border : 2px dashed RoyalBlue ; }
```

4 Now, add rules to specify the appearance of the flex items
```
div.flex-container > div {
        padding : 10px 40px ;
        background : LightSteelBlue ;
        border : 2px solid RoyalBlue ;
        font : 1.25em sans-serif ; }
```

5 Save the HTML document, then open it in a web browser to see the flexbox layout

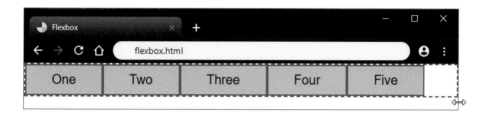

6 Drag one side of the browser window to make it narrower and see the layout wrap flex items onto the next row

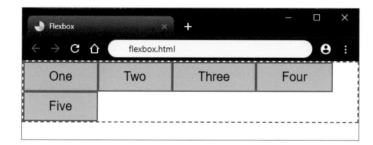

7 Edit the rules in Step 3 – to reverse the wrapping order

```
div.flex-container {        display : flex ;
                           flex-wrap : wrap-reverse ;
                           background : RoyalBlue ; }
```

8 Save the HTML document again, then refresh the web browser to see the flex items appear in reverse order

The default value for the **wrap** property is **nowrap**.

Direct Flexbox

CSS provides a **flex-direction** property that, by default, has a **row** value, but you can reverse the order of flex items on a row by specifying a **row-reverse** value to the **flex-direction** property. Alternatively, flex items can appear in a column by specifying a **column** or **column-reverse** value to the **flex-direction** property.

To have flex items wrap to the next row or column, you can add a **flex-wrap : wrap ;** rule, as in the previous example on pages 132-133, or you can use a **flex-flow** shorthand property to concisely specify values for both **flex-direction** and **flex-wrap** – for example, **flex-flow : column wrap ;** to have the flex items appear in wrapping columns.

If you want to arrange the flex items in a specific order, you can reference each inner "child" element by specifying its index number in the parentheses of an **:nth-child( )** pseudo-class selector, and specify your preferred index number to an **order** property.

direct.html

1 Create an HTML document with a division element that contains five inner divisions
```
<div class="flex-container">
        <div>One</div>
        <div>Two</div>
        <div>Three</div>
        <div>Four</div>
        <div>Five</div>
</div>
```

2 Add a style sheet with rules to control the web page
```
* { margin : 0 ; padding : 0 ; box-sizing : border-box ; }
```

Notice that a height is specified, otherwise the browser will allow scrolling down the flexible column.

3 Next, add rules to make the outer division flexible
```
div.flex-container {        display : flex ;
                            flex-flow : column wrap ;
                            border : 2px dashed RoyalBlue ;
                            height : 200px ; }
```

4 Now, add rules to specify the appearance of the flex items
```
div.flex-container > div {
        padding : 10px 40px ; background : LightSteelBlue ;
        border : 2px solid RoyalBlue ;
        font : 1.25em sans-serif ; }
```

5 Save the HTML document, then open it in a web browser to see the flexbox direction

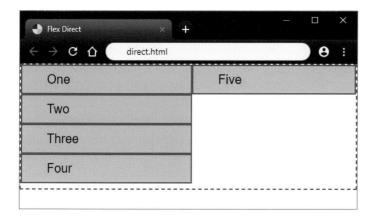

6 Now, add rules to specify a preferred index number for each flex item to change their order

div.flex-container **> div:nth-child(1) { order : 3 ; }**

div.flex-container **> div:nth-child(2) { order : 4 ; }**

div.flex-container **> div:nth-child(3) { order : 5 ; }**

div.flex-container **> div:nth-child(4) { order : 2 ; }**

div.flex-container **> div:nth-child(5) { order : 1 ; }**

7 Save the HTML document again, then refresh the web browser to see the flex items appear in a specific order

Changing the flex item order only changes the visual appearance, not the element's index number in the Document Object Model (DOM) – so may cause confusion when referencing the elements in JavaScript.

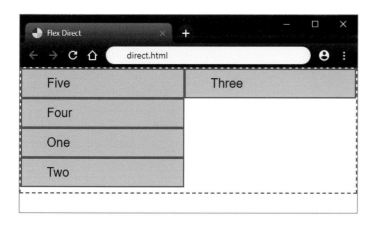

Align Items

The flexbox examples on pages 132-134 have stretched the flex items within the confines of their lines in the flex container. This is the default behavior, but you can control how the flex items align along their lines using a CSS **justify-content** property to specify **center, flex-start, flex-end, space-evenly, space-around,** or **space-between**. The **center** value aligns items around the center of the line, but **flex-start** and **flex-end** aligns them at the start or end of the container. The **space-evenly** value adds even space around each item; **space-around** adds space between, but half-space before and after the items; and **space-between** only adds space between.

You can also control how the flex items align vertically within their lines using an **align-items** property to specify **center, flex-start** (start of the line), or **flex-end** (end of the line).

Similarly, you can control how the lines align within the flex container using an **align-content** property to specify **center, flex-start** (start of the container) or **flex-end** (end of the container).

If you want to align individual flex items vertically within their line, you can reference each inner child element by specifying its index number in the parentheses of an **:nth-child( )** pseudo-class selector, and specify your preferred value to an **align-self** property.

Hot tip

For perfect centering use **justify-content : center ; align-items : center ;** style rules.

HTML

alignment.html

1 Create an HTML document with a division element that contains five inner divisions
```
<div class="flex-container">
        <div>One</div>
        <div>Two</div>
        <div>Three</div>
        <div>Four</div>
        <div>Five</div>
</div>
```

2 Add a style sheet with rules to control the web page
```
* { margin : 0 ; padding : 0 ; box-sizing : border-box ; }
```

3 Next, add rules to make the outer division flexible and specify how the flex items should align
```
div.flex-container { display : flex ; flex-flow : row wrap ;
                     border : 2px dashed RoyalBlue ;
                     height : 200px ;
                     justify-content : space-between ;
                     align-items : center ; }
```

4 Now, add rules to specify the appearance of the flex items
```
div.flex-container > div {
        padding : 10px 40px ; background : LightSteelBlue ;
        border : 2px solid RoyalBlue ;
        font : 1.25em sans-serif ; }
```

5 Save the HTML document, then open it in a web browser to see the flex item alignment

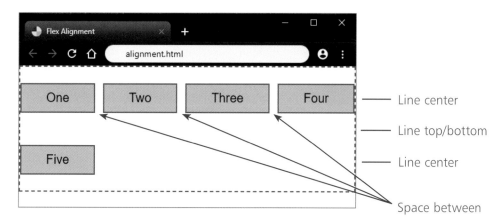

— Line center

— Line top/bottom

— Line center

— Space between

6 Now, add rules to change the alignment of two flex items
```
div.flex-container > div:nth-child( 2 ) { align-self : flex-end ; }
div.flex-container > div:nth-child( 3 ) { align-self : flex-start ; }
```

Don't forget

7 Save the HTML document again, then refresh the web browser to see the changed flex items alignment

The **align-self** property overrides the alignment specified to the **align-items** property.

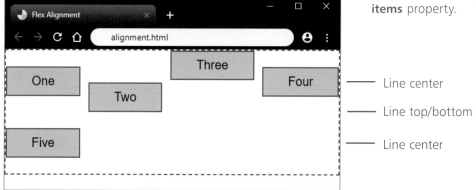

— Line center

— Line top/bottom

— Line center

Manage Resizing

CSS provides properties that let you control the size and flexibility of flex items. You can specify a size to a **flex-basis** property to specify the initial length of a flex item, and specify a value of **1** to both **flex-grow** and **flex-shrink** properties – to allow them to grow and shrink to fill a flex container.

Conversely, if you specify a value of **0** to the **flex-shrink** property, you disallow the flex item's ability to shrink, and specifying a number greater than one to the **flex-grow** property allows a flex item to grow more than other flex items that have a value of **1**.

There is a shorthand **flex** property that can be used to specify values for **flex-grow**, **flex-shrink** and **flex-basis** values concisely.

resize.html

1 Create an HTML document with two division elements that each contains three inner divisions
```
<div class="flex-container top">
  <div>One</div><div>Two</div><div>Three</div>
</div>
```

```
<div class="flex-container btm">
  <div>One</div><div>Two</div><div>Three</div>
</div>
```

2 Add a style sheet with rules to control the web page
```
* { margin : 0 ; padding : 0 ; box-sizing : border-box ; }
```

3 Next, add rules to make the outer divisions flexible
```
div.flex-container {      display : flex ;
                         margin: 20px ;
                         border : 2px dashed RoyalBlue ; }
```

4 Now, add rules to specify the appearance of the flex items
```
div.flex-container > div {
                         padding : 30px 20px ;
                         background : LightSteelBlue ;
                         border : 2px solid RoyalBlue ;
                         font : 1.25em sans-serif ; }
```

5 Then, add rules to specify the initial size of each flex item and allow them all to grow and shrink
```
div.top > div { flex : 1 1 50px ; }
div.btm > div { flex : 1 1 250px ; }
```

6 Save the HTML document again, then open it in a web browser to see the flex items fill each flex container

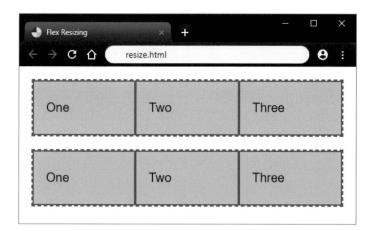

7 Now, add rules to allow one flex item greater growth, and disallow one flex item's ability to shrink
div.top > div:nth-child(3) { flex-grow : 5 ; }
div.btm > div:nth-child(2) { flex-shrink : 0 ; }

8 Save the HTML document again, then refresh the web browser to see the resized flex items

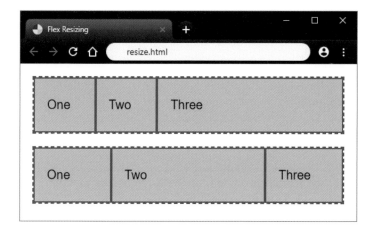

The value specified to **flex-grow** determines how far it will grow relative to the other flex items – you can increase the number to see it grow more.

Query Media

CSS has the ability to discover the capabilities of the viewing device by making "media queries" to apply appropriate style rules. The syntax of a CSS media query looks like this:

@media *media-type* **and (** *media-feature* **) {** *style-rules* **}**

The media type can be specified using any of the keywords below:

Keyword:	Description:
all	Detect all media types
print	Detect printers
screen	Detect PC desktop, tablet, and phone screens
speech	Detect screenreaders

A media query can check for many types of media feature, but the most useful are those that detect the width of the display area and orientation of the device using these keywords:

Keyword:	Description:
min-width	Minimum width of the display area, such as the width of the browser window
max-width	Maximum width of the display area, such as the width of the browser window
orientation	Orientation of the viewport, as either landscape mode or portrait mode

Hot tip

A media query can check for the existence of multiple media features by adding further **and (** *media-feature* **)** parts to the query.

When a specified media feature is detected on the specified media type, the media query will report as true, so style rules within its curly brackets will be applied – otherwise they will be ignored. For example, to apply a background color only on devices whose display area is 600 pixels wide or less with this media query:

```
@media screen and ( max-width:600px ) {
        body { background : Blue ; }
}
```

...cont'd

1 Create an HTML document with a style sheet that specifies a default background color for wide display areas

```
body { background : Tomato ; }
```

mediaquery.html

2 Next, add a media query to specify a background color for medium-width display areas

```
@media screen and ( min-width:600px )
                    and ( max-width:992px ) {
  body { background : DarkOrange ; }
}
```

Notice that there are no spaces around the colon character in the media-feature specifications.

3 Now, add media queries for small-width display areas and different orientations

```
@media screen and ( max-width:600px )
                    and ( orientation:landscape ) {
     body { background : LimeGreen ; }
}

@media screen and ( max-width:600px )
                    and ( orientation:portrait ) {
     body { background : RoyalBlue ; }
}
```

4 Save the HTML document then open it in desktop, tablet, and cellphone devices to see appropriate colors

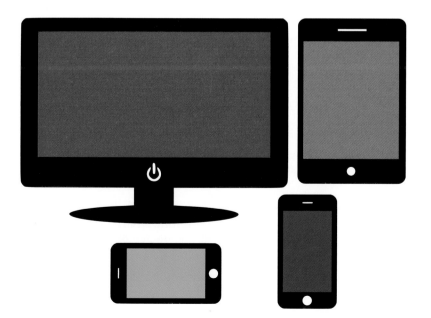

The values specified for screen widths here are typical breakpoints used to target small, medium, and large devices.

Switch Navigation

Media queries allow appropriate navigation to be provided for large and small devices. Typically, a horizontal navigation bar is provided for wide display areas, whereas a vertical navigation list is more suitable for smaller screens.

Vertical navigation bars will specify a fixed **width** value for the list, whereas horizontal navigation bars can instead **float** the list items and hide the **overflow** to maintain the visibility of the bar.

medianav.html

1 Create an HTML document containing a list with four hyperlink items
```
<ul>
<li><a href="#home" class="current">Home</a></li>
<li><a href="#info">Information</a></li>
<li><a href="#extra">Extra</a></li>
<li><a href="#contact">Contact</a></li>
</ul>
```

2 Add a style sheet with rules to control the web page
```
* { margin : 0 ; padding : 0 ; box-sizing : border-box ; }
```

3 Next, add rules to remove the markers, margin, and padding, then specify a color, fixed width, and font
```
ul {    list-style-type : none ;
        margin : 0 ;
        padding : 0 ;
        background : LightSteelBlue ;
        width : 150px ;
        font : 1.25em sans-serif ; }
```

4 Now, add style rules to display the hyperlinks in blocks and specify how they should appear
```
li a {    display : block ;
          text-align : center ;
          text-decoration : none ;
          color : Black ;
          padding : 10px ; }
```

5 Then, add style rules to indicate the hyperlinks' status
```
li a.current { background : CornflowerBlue ; }
li a:hover { background : RoyalBlue ; color : White ; }
```

6 Finally, add a media query that will apply new rules when the display area is 600 pixels or more in width
@media screen and (min-width:600px) {

      ul { overflow : hidden ; width : 100% ; }
      li a { float : left ; }

}

7 Save the HTML document then open the web page in a desktop web browser to see the horizontal navigation bar

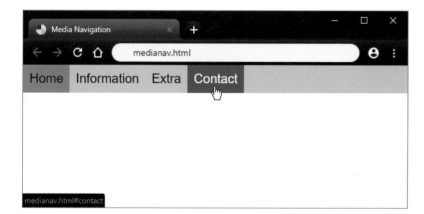

This example is similar to that on pages 90-91, but automates the switch of navigation type.

143

8 Drag the edge of the browser to reduce its size to see the navigation bar automatically switch to a vertical list

Summary

- A universal style rule can be used to override the browser's default styles for **margin** and **padding**.

- An element's total width and height is unaffected by the addition of an **outline**.

- Elements that can be resized should specify how to handle any content **overflow**.

- A **column-count** can specify the number of columns into which text content should be divided.

- A **column-gap** can specify the gutter width between columns.

- A **column-rule** shorthand can specify the width, style, and color of a vertical ruled line to appear between columns.

- A **column-span** can specify the number of columns to span.

- The flexible box scheme first requires a flex container element be created by specifying a **flex** value to its **display** property.

- Inner elements within a **flex** container are flex items that will appear on a single row by default.

- A **flex-wrap** can specify whether a row of flex items should wrap onto the next line.

- A **flex-direction** can specify whether flex items should appear in rows or columns.

- A **justify-content** can align flex items horizontally, and an **align-items** can align flex items vertically on the line.

- A **flex** shorthand can specify the initial length of a flex item and whether they may grow or shrink to fill a flex container.

- A media query can be used to discover the capabilities of the viewing device to apply appropriate style rules.

- A media query can specify a **screen** media type to detect PC desktop, tablet, and phone screens.

- A media query can check for many types of media feature to discover the display area's width, and **orientation** of the device.

7 Import & Script Style Sheets

Create Content

CSS style rules can be written between HTML **<style>** **</style>** tags, as are most examples in this book, or in an external style sheet imported using the HTML **<link>** tag – as described on page 13.

Additionally, CSS provides an **@import** rule that allows style sheets to be imported into other style sheets by specifying the style sheet's file name (or file name and path) to the CSS **url( )** function – for example, **@import url(more-styles.css) ;**.

Crucially, the **@import** rule must appear at the very top of the style sheet into which the style rules are to be imported, or on the first line between **<style>** **</style>** tags in an HTML document.

JavaScript can also be used to dynamically add new style sheets to an HTML document, and JavaScript can be used to choose which style sheets to enable or disable.

By importing several style sheets you can provide different styling of an HTML document to suit the user's preference. In order to demonstrate this ability, this chapter will develop a simple web page that provides various styles by importing four style sheets and one dynamically created by JavaScript. The first stage of development is to create the HTML content of the web page:

content.html

1 Create an HTML document containing a page heading
<h1>Cascading Style Sheets</h1>

2 Next, add an unordered list containing links that target some JavaScript functions
<ul>
<li><a href="javascript:applyStyle(1)">1-Column</a></li>

<li><a href="javascript:applyStyle(2)">2-Column</a></li>

<li><a href="javascript:applyStyle(3)">3-Column</a></li>

<li><a href="javascript:darkMode( )">Dark Mode</a></li>
</ul>

3 Now, below the list, add a sub-heading
<h2>What is CSS?</h2>

4 Then, add the main content of the web page

```
<main>
<p>
<span id="first">
Cascading Style Sheets are used to control the
presentational aspects of HTML documents.
</span>

<span id="second">
CSS was created by the World Wide Web consortium to
regain control of document markup.
</span>
</p>

<aside>The World Wide Web Consortium (W3C) oversees
web standards.
</aside>
</main>
```

The **id** attribute values will be used later to style the **<span>** elements.

5 Finally, add a footer to the bottom of the web page

```
<footer>
<p>Styled by CSS in easy steps</p>
</footer>
```

6 Save the HTML document, then open it in a web browser – it should look like the screenshot below

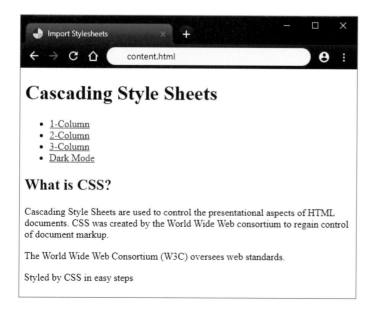

Base Navigation

To develop the simple web page created on pages 146-147, the next stage is to override the browser's default styles with custom styles that provide a navigation bar:

base[0].css

1 Begin an external style sheet with rules to control the page
`* { margin : 0 ; padding : 0 ; box-sizing : border-box ; }`

2 Next, add a rule to provide a left margin to all elements – except the unordered list
`h1, h2, main, footer { margin : 0 0 0 5px ; }`

3 Now, add rules to make the list into a navigation bar
```
ul {
        list-style-type : none ;
        margin : 0 ;
        padding : 0 ;
        background : Thistle ;
        font : 1em sans-serif ;
        width : 100% ;
        overflow : hidden ; }
```

4 Then, add rules to style the hyperlinks
```
li a {
        display : block ;
        text-align : center ;
        text-decoration : none ;
        color : Black ;
        padding : 10px ;
        float : left ; }
```

Hot tip

The **:last-child selector** is yet another pseudo-class. It selects the final inner element within an outer containing element.

5 Finally, add rules to indicate when the user places the cursor over any link, and to position the final hyperlink at the far right
`li a:hover { background : Purple ; color : White ; }`

`li:last-child { float : right ; }`

6 Save the external style sheet as a file named "base[0].css" in the same folder location as the HTML document created on pages 146-147

7 Next, make a new copy of the HTML document, and save it as "base.html" alongside the **base[0].css** style sheet

base.html

8 Insert this **<style>** element, immediately after the **<title>** element, in the new HTML document's head section

```
<style>
@import url( base[0].css ) ;
</style>
```

9 Save the new HTML document, then open it in a web browser to see the imported styles get applied

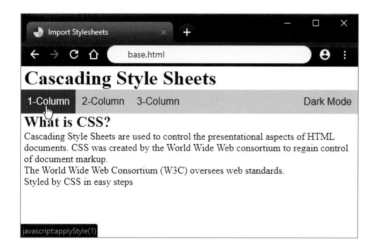

You can place the mouse over any hyperlink button to see its colors change – but clicking a button will do nothing at this stage.

When the web browser loads a web page that contains style sheets it adds them internally to a document "styleSheets" list object in the Document Object Model (DOM). This is an index-numbered list, starting from zero, to which the style sheets are added in the top-to-bottom order that the browser reads ("parses") them.

In JavaScript, the first style sheet parsed can be referenced as **document.styleSheets[0]**, the second style sheet parsed as **document.styleSheets[1]**, and so on.

The numbering in the file names given to the external style sheets in this example do not dictate the list order, but are merely reminders of the order in which they are added to the HTML document – so they will be added to the document "styleSheets" list object in the same order for easy recognition in JavaScript.

Notice that the capitalization of the **styleSheets** object name uses the "camelCase" naming convention and cannot be written as **document.stylesheets**.

Single Column

To further develop the simple web page on page 149, the next stage is to add styles that color the headings and footer, indicate the current page style to the user, and insert quote marks around the aside comment:

single[1].css

1 Begin an external style sheet with a rule to provide the navigation bar – created by the earlier style sheet
@import url(base[0].css) ;

2 Next, add a rule to color both headings
h1, h2 { color : MediumPurple ; }

3 Now, add rules to style the footer in smaller colored italic font
footer {
        padding : 10px 0 ;
        font : italic 0.75em sans-serif ;
        color : MediumPurple ; }

4 Then, add rules to indicate the current page style
li:nth-child(1) > a {
        background : MediumPurple ;
        color : White ; }

5 Finally, add rules to insert quote marks around the aside comment
aside:before { content : open-quote ; }

aside:after { content : close-quote ; }

6 Save the external style sheet as a file named "single[1].css" in the same folder location as the HTML document created on page 149

7   Next, make a new copy of the HTML document, and save it as "single.html" alongside the **single[1].css** style sheet

single.html

8   Insert another **<style>** element in the new HTML document's head section, immediately after the previous one – so it now looks like this:

```
<style>
@import url( base[0].css ) ;
</style>

<style>
@import url( single[1].css ) ;
</style>
```

9   Save the new HTML document, then open it in a web browser to see all imported styles get applied

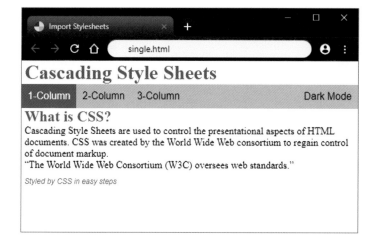

Notice that the first hyperlink button is now colored to indicate the current layout is single column – but clicking a button will have no response until some JavaScript code is added.

Although the navigation style rules are now imported both in the first **<style>** element and in the second style sheet, the navigation style will be maintained later simply by applying individual style sheets from JavaScript code.

Add JavaScript

To continue developing the simple web page on page 151, the next stage is to add some JavaScript code that will apply particular style sheet rules when the user chooses an option on the navigation bar:

script.html

1 Copy the previous HTML document and add a **<script>** **</script>** element just before the closing **</body>** tag

2 Begin the script by inserting code inside the **<script>** element to dynamically add a style sheet to the document

```
let node = document.createElement( "style" ) ;
node.innerText =
"h1{ color:Lime; } body{ background:Black; color:White; }" ;
document.head.appendChild( node ) ;
```

3 Create a reference to the dynamically-added style sheet

```
let sheet =
document.styleSheets[ document.styleSheets.length-1 ] ;
```

4 Next, add a function to apply or discard the rules in the dynamically-added style sheet in response to a user action

```
function darkMode( ) {
  sheet.disabled=( sheet.disabled===true ) ? false : true ;
}
```

5 Now, add a function to apply or discard the rules in other style sheets in response to a user action

```
function applyStyle( n ) {
  for ( let i = 0 ; i < document.styleSheets.length ; i++ )
  { document.styleSheets[ i ].disabled = true ; }
  document.styleSheets[ n ].disabled = false ;
}
```

6 Add a function call just before the **</script>** tag to apply the document's second style sheet when this page loads

```
applyStyle( 1 ) ;
```

Hot tip

The length of the **styleSheets** object list is the total number of style sheets in the document, but because the list is numbered from zero, the final style sheet is numbered one less than the list's length. For example, where there is a total of three style sheets, the final one is index number 2.

7 Save the new HTML document as "script.html", alongside the style sheets, then open it in a web browser to see the imported styles get applied by the script code

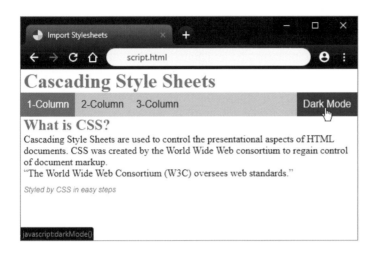

8 Click the final hyperlink button on the navigation bar to apply the style rules in the dynamically-added style sheet

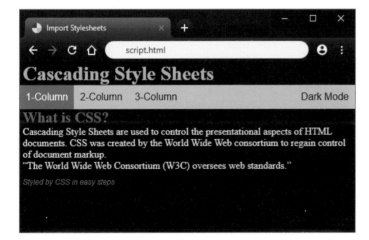

Hot tip

You can also click the first hyperlink button to discard the rules in the dynamically-added style sheet – by applying the style rules in the **single[1].css** style sheet.

9 Click the button once more to discard the style rules in the dynamically-added style sheet

Twin Column

The next stage in the development of the simple web page on pages 146-153 is to add styles that will change the layout of the main content to two columns when the user chooses an option on the navigation bar:

twin[2].css

1 Begin an external style sheet with a rule to provide the navigation bar – created by the earlier style sheet
@import url(base[0].css) ;

2 Next, add a rule to color both headings
h1, h2 { color : MediumPurple ; }

3 Now, add rules to style the footer in smaller colored italic font
footer {
　　　　padding : 10px 0 ;
　　　　font : italic 0.75em sans-serif ;
　　　　color : MediumPurple ; }

4 Then, add rules to indicate the current page style
li:nth-child(2) > a {
　　　　background : MediumPurple ;
　　　　color : White ; }

5 Finally, add rules to float two sections of the main content
main > p {
　　　　float : left ;
　　　　width : 70% ;
　　　　border-right : 1px solid MediumPurple ; }

aside　　{
　　　　float : left ;
　　　　width : 30% ;
　　　　padding-left : 10px ; }

footer　{ clear : both ; }

6 Save the external style sheet as a file named "twin[2].css" in the same folder location as the HTML document created on page 153

7 Next, make a new copy of the HTML document, and save it as "twin.html" alongside the **twin[2].css** style sheet

twin.html

8 Insert another **<style>** element in the new HTML document's head section, immediately after the previous one – so it now looks like this:

```
<style>
@import url( base[0].css ) ;
</style>

<style>
@import url( single[1].css ) ;
</style>

<style>
@import url( twin[2].css ) ;
</style>
```

9 Save the new HTML document, then open it and click the second hyperlink button on the navigation bar to apply the style rules in the latest style sheet

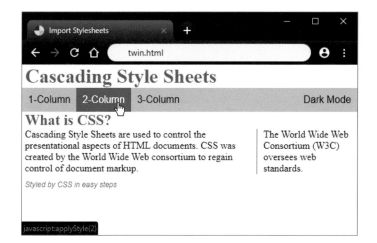

You can also click the final button on the navigation bar to toggle between modes in either single-column or two-column layout.

10 Click the first hyperlink button on the navigation bar to apply the style rules in the earlier style sheet – switching back to a single-column layout

Triple Column

The final stage in the development of the simple web page on pages 146-155 is to add styles that will change the layout of the main content to three columns when the user chooses an option on the navigation bar:

triple[3].css

1 Begin an external style sheet with a rule to provide the navigation bar – created by the earlier style sheet
@import url(base[0].css) ;

2 Next, add rules to color and position headings
h1, h2 { color : MediumPurple ; }
h1   { text-align : center ; }

3 Now, add rules to style the footer in colored italic font
**footer { padding : 10px 0 ; font : italic 0.75em sans-serif ;
           color : MediumPurple ; }**

4 Then, add rules to indicate the current page style
**li:nth-child(3) > a {
           background : MediumPurple ; color : White ; }**

5 Finally, add rules to float three sections of the content
**span#first {
           float : left ;
           width : 30% ;
           border-right : 1px solid MediumPurple ;
           padding-right : 5px ; }**

**span#second {
           float : left ;
           width : 40% ;
           border-right : 1px solid MediumPurple ;
           padding : 0 10px ; }**

aside   { float : left ; width : 30% ; padding-left : 10px ; }

footer   { clear : both ; text-align : center ;   }

6 Save the external style sheet as a file named "triple[3].css" in the same folder location as the HTML document created on page 155

7 Next, make a new copy of the HTML document, and save it as "triple.html" alongside the **triple[3].css** style sheet

triple.html

8 Insert another **<style>** element in the new HTML document's head section, immediately after the previous one – so it now looks like this:

```
<style>
@import url( base[0].css ) ;
</style>

<style>
@import url( single[1].css ) ;
</style>

<style>
@import url( twin[2].css ) ;
</style>

<style>
@import url( triple[3].css ) ;
</style>
```

9 Save the new HTML document, then click the third hyperlink button on the navigation bar to apply the style rules in the final style sheet

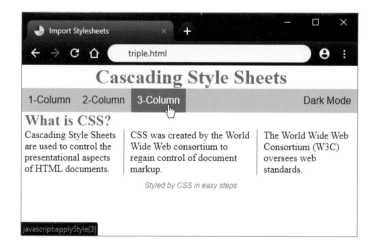

Don't forget

You can also click the button on the right of the navigation bar to toggle between modes in any layout.

10 Click any of the buttons on the left of the navigation bar to apply style rules from an external style sheet

Summary

- The CSS **@import** rule allows style sheets to be imported into other style sheets using the CSS **url( )** function.

- An **@import** rule must appear at top of the style sheet or on the first line of a style element.

- The final element within a containing element can be selected using the **:last-child** pseudo-class selector.

- The web browser adds style sheets to a **document.styleSheets** list object in the Document Object Model (DOM).

- The **document.styleSheets** list object is index-numbered starting from zero.

- Style sheets are added to the **document.styleSheets** list in the top-to-bottom order that the browser parses them.

- The first style sheet in the **document.styleSheets** list can be referenced in script as **document.styleSheets[0]**.

- The length of the **document.styleSheets** list object is the total number of style sheets in the HTML document.

- The index number of the final style sheet in the **document.styleSheets** list is always one less than its length.

- JavaScript can be used to dynamically add new style sheets to an HTML document.

- The JavaScript **document.createElement( )** function can be used to create a **<style>** element.

- The JavaScript **innerText** property of an element can be used to add style rules.

- The JavaScript **document.head.appendChild( )** function can be used to add an element to the head section of a document.

- The **disabled** property of a style sheet can be used to apply or discard its style rules.

- Multiple style sheets can be provided to allow the user to choose a preferred web page layout and page mode.

8 Design with Grids

Draw Grid

The CSS flexible box "flexbox" layout scheme, described in Chapter 6, is a 1-dimensional system, which can automatically wrap its flex item lines to the next row or column in small display areas.

By contrast, the CSS grid layout scheme is a 2-dimensional system, which places "grid items" in columns and rows.

To create a grid layout you must first define an element to be a "grid container" by specifying a **grid** (or **inline-grid**) value to its **display** property. All direct child elements within a grid container then automatically become the grid items.

A **grid** is block-level, so will fill the page width, whereas an **inline-grid** does not do so.

When creating a large number of columns, you can use a **repeat( )** function to concisely specify how many **fr** fragments are required – for example, to create a grid with 10 columns **grid-template-columns : repeat(10, 1fr) ;** (see page 177).

You specify how many columns the grid should have as a space-separated list of width values to a **grid-template-columns** property, or using an **auto** keyword to automatically size the column width. Specify **auto** for each column if you want the columns to have the same width – for example, for a grid with three columns specify this rule: **grid-template-columns : auto auto auto ;**
If there are more grid items than the number of specified columns, the grid will automatically add another row to accommodate them.

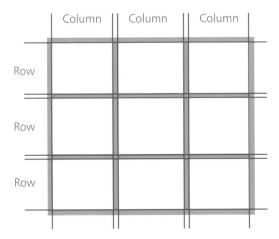

Similarly, you can specify how many rows the grid should have as a space-separated list of height values to a **grid-template-rows** property, or using the **auto** keyword to automatically size the row height. Specify **auto** for each row if you want the rows to have the same height – for example, for a grid with three rows specify this rule: **grid-template-rows : auto auto auto ;**
If there are more grid items than the number of specified rows, the grid will automatically add another column to accommodate them.

...cont'd

1 Create an HTML document with a division element containing seven inner divisions

```html
<div class="grid-container">
  <div>One</div> <div>Two</div> <div>Three</div>
  <div>Four</div> <div>Five</div> <div>Six</div>
  <div>Seven</div>
</div>
```

grid.html

2 Add a style sheet with rules to control the web page

```css
* { margin : 0 ; padding : 0 ; box-sizing : border-box ; }
```

3 Next, add rules to make the outer division into a grid of three columns and two rows

```css
div.grid-container {
  display : grid ;
  grid-template-columns : auto 250px auto ;
  grid-template-rows : auto 100px ;
  border : 2px dashed DeepSkyBlue ; }
```

All modern browsers support grid layout since:

 Chrome 57.0

 Edge 16.0

 Firefox 52.0

Safari 10

O Opera 44

4 Now, add rules to specify the appearance of the grid items

```css
div.grid-container > div {
  background : LightBlue ;
  border : 2px solid DeepSkyBlue ;
  padding : 10px 40px ;
  font : 1.25em sans-serif ; }
```

161

5 Save the HTML document, then open it in a web browser to see the grid layout

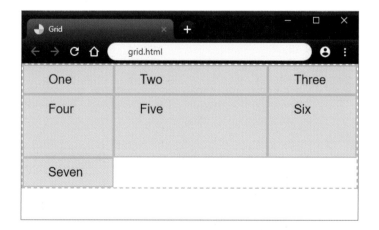

Notice that the second row and column is larger, and a third row is automatically added. Subsequent rows would all use only the first row template values.

Align Items

The grid layout example on pages 160-161 has stretched the grid items within the confines of their lines in the grid container. This is the default behavior, but you can control how the grid items align along their lines using a CSS **justify-content** property to specify **center**, **start**, **end**, **space-evenly**, **space-around**, or **space-between**. The **center** value aligns items around the center of the grid container, but **start** and **end** aligns them at the start or end of the container. The **space-evenly** value adds even space around each item; **space-around** adds space between, but half-space before and after the items; and **space-between** only adds space between.

You can also control how the grid items align vertically within their lines using an **align-items** property to specify **center**, **start** (start of the cell), or **end** (end of the cell).

Similarly, you can control how the lines align within the grid container using an **align-content** property to specify **center**, **start** (start of the container), or **end** (end of the container).

If you want to align individual grid items vertically within their line, you can reference each inner child element by specifying its index number in the parentheses of an **:nth-child( )** pseudo-class selector and specify your preferred value to an **align-self** property.

The **justify-content** property is only useful when the overall width of the grid is less than the width of the grid's container.

gridalign.html

1. Create an HTML document with a division element that contains five inner divisions
```
<div class="grid-container">
  <div>One</div>
  <div>Two</div>
  <div>Three</div>
  <div>Four</div>
  <div>Five</div>
</div>
```

2. Add a style sheet with rules to control the web page
```
* { margin : 0 ; padding : 0 ; box-sizing : border-box ; }
```

3. Next, add rules to make the outer division into a grid container and specify how the grid items should align
```
div.grid-container {
  display : grid ; height : 200px ;
  grid-template-columns : auto auto auto auto ;
  justify-content : space-between ; align-items : center ;
  border : 2px dashed DeepSkyBlue ; }
```

4 Now, add rules to specify the appearance of the grid items
```
div.grid-container > div {
  padding : 10px 40px ; background : LightBlue ;
  border : 2px solid DeepSkyBlue ;
  font : 1.25em sans-serif ; }
```

5 Save the HTML document, then open it in a web browser to see the grid item alignment

This layout replicates that of the flexbox example on pages 136-137 – but when you expand the browser width, flexbox will unwrap its items, whereas the grid maintains its item layout.

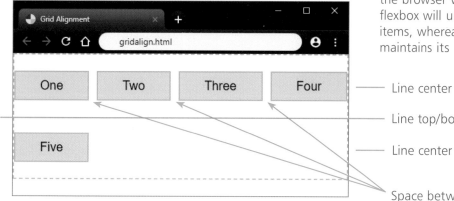

Line center

Line top/bottom

Line center

Space between

163

6 Now, add rules to change the alignment of two flex items
```
div.grid-container > div:nth-child( 2 ) { align-self : end ; }
div.grid-container > div:nth-child( 3 ) { align-self : start ; }
```

7 Save the HTML document again, then refresh the web browser to see the changed grid items alignment

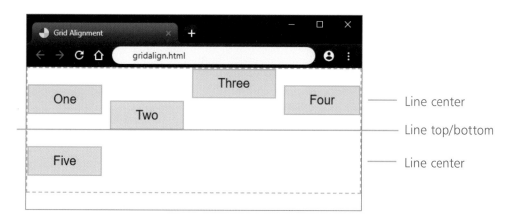

Line center

Line top/bottom

Line center

Mind Gaps

With grid containers, the space between the columns and rows are known as "gaps". More specifically, the spaces between rows are "row gaps", and the spaces between columns are "column gaps".

You can assign a size value to a CSS **grid-column-gap** property to specify the width of the column gaps, and assign a size value to a CSS **grid-row-gap** property to specify the height of the row gaps. If no **grid-row-gap** is specified, its value will be set to that of the **grid-column-gap** property.

There is also a **grid-gap** shorthand property that can be used to specify both row height and column width by assigning a single value for uniform gaps, or by assigning two space-separated values to specify row height and column width – in that order.

Gap sizing can be used in conjunction with the **justify-content**, **align-items**, and **align-content** properties, introduced in the previous example on pages 162-163, to align the grid items within a grid container. Specified gaps are added <u>between</u> the edges of any existing space between the columns and rows, not on the edge of the grid items.

The **grid-** prefix will be removed from all three of these property names in the CSS specifications. At the time of writing, some modern browsers already support **row-gap**, **column-gap**, and **gap** property names instead.

gridgaps.html

1 Create an HTML document with a division element that contains six inner divisions
```
<div class="grid-container">
  <div>One</div> <div>Two</div> <div>Three</div>
  <div>Four</div> <div>Five</div> <div>Six</div>
</div>
```

2 Add a style sheet with rules to control the web page
```
* { margin : 0 ; padding : 0 ; box-sizing : border-box ; }
```

3 Next, add rules to make the outer division into a grid container and specify how the grid items should align
```
div.grid-container {
  display : grid ; height : 200px ;
  grid-template-columns : 100px 100px 100px ;
  grid-template-rows : 100px 100px ;

  justify-content : space-evenly ;
  align-items : center ;
  align-content : center ;

  border : 2px dashed DeepSkyBlue ; }
```

4 Now, add rules to specify the appearance of the grid items
div.grid-container > div {
  padding : 10px 30px ; background : LightBlue ;
  border : 2px solid DeepSkyBlue ;
  font : 1.25em sans-serif ; }

5 Save the HTML document, then open it in a web
browser to see the grid item alignment

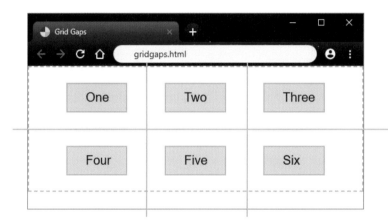

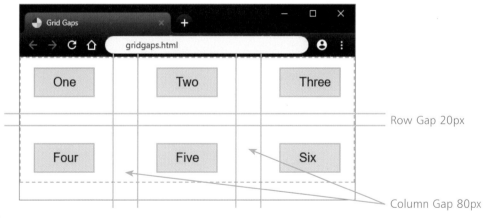

6 Now, add rules to add gaps between columns and rows
div.grid-container {
  grid-column-gap : 80px ; grid-row-gap : 20px ; }

7 Save the HTML document once more, then refresh the
browser to see the gaps added to the grid item alignment

Place Items

With grid containers, the lines at the leading edge between the columns and rows are known as "column lines" and "row lines".

Line numbers can be used to place grid items at a specific position in a grid container. You can assign a column line number to **grid-column-start** and

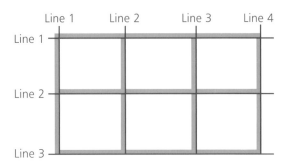

grid-column-end properties to specify the horizontal position and extent of a grid item. Similarly, **grid-row-start** and **grid-row-end** properties can each be assigned row line numbers to specify the vertical position and extent of a grid item.

There are also **grid-column** and **grid-row** shorthand properties that can be used to specify horizontal and vertical positioning. Each are specified by assigning two "/" forward slash-separated values to specify start and end – in that order.

gridlines.html

1 Create an HTML document with a division element that contains three inner divisions
```
<div class="grid-container">
  <div>One</div> <div>Two</div> <div>Three</div>
</div>
```

2 Add a style sheet with rules to control the web page and to make the outer division into a grid container
```
* { margin : 0 ; padding : 0 ; box-sizing : border-box ; }

div.grid-container {
  display : grid ; height : 200px ;
  grid-template-columns : 100px 100px 100px ;
  grid-template-rows : 100px 100px ;
  justify-content : space-evenly ;
  align-items : center ; align-content : center ;
  border : 2px dashed DeepSkyBlue ; }
```

3 Now, add rules to specify the appearance of the grid items
```
div.grid-container > div {
  padding : 10px 30px ; background : LightBlue ;
  border : 2px solid DeepSkyBlue ; font : 1.25em sans-serif ; }
```

4 Save the HTML document, then open it in a web browser to see the grid item alignment

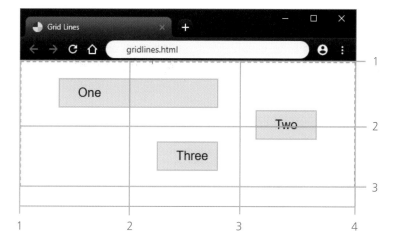

5 Now, add rules to place each one of the grid items
div.grid-container > div:nth-child(1) {
  grid-column : 1 / 3 ; **grid-row** : 1 / 2 ; }

div.grid-container > div:nth-child(2) {
  grid-column : 3 / 4 ; **grid-row** : 1 / 3 ; }

div.grid-container > div:nth-child(3) {
  grid-column : 2 / 3 ; **grid-row** : 2 / 3 ; }

6 Save the HTML document once more, then refresh the browser to see the position and extent of the grid items

Define Areas

Entire areas of a grid container can be defined by specifying a "/" forward slash-separated list of line numbers, introduced in the previous example on pages 166-167, to a **grid-area** property. This is a shorthand property for the **grid-row-start**, **grid-column-start**, **grid-row-end**, **grid-column-end** properties. The specified values effectively describe two diagonally opposed coordinates of a rectangular area.

For example, **grid-area : 1 / 2 / 2 / 4 ;** describes a top-left coordinate at row 1, column 2, and a bottom-right coordinate at row 2, column 4.

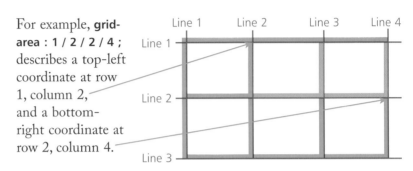

The **grid-area** property can also be used to assign names to grid items. Usefully, the names given to grid items can be specified to a **grid-template-areas** property within single quote marks, which represent the columns and rows of the grid container.

gridareas.html

1 Create an HTML document with a division element that contains five inner divisions
```
<div class="grid-container">
  <div>Head</div> <div>Menu</div> <div>Main</div>
  <div>Aside</div> <div>Foot</div>
</div>
```

2 Add a style sheet with rules to control the web page and to make the outer division into a grid container
```
* { margin : 0 ; padding : 0 ; box-sizing : border-box ; }

div.grid-container {
  display : grid ; height : 200px ;
  grid-template-columns : 20% auto auto auto 20% ;
  grid-template-rows : 20% auto 20% ;
  border : 2px dashed DeepSkyBlue ; }
```

3 Now, add rules to specify the appearance of the grid items
```
div.grid-container > div {
  padding : 10px 30px ; background : LightBlue ;
  border : 2px solid DeepSkyBlue ; font : 1.25em sans-serif ; }
```

4 Save the HTML document, then open it in a web browser to see the grid item alignment

5 Now, add rules to name each of the grid items
```
div.grid-container > div:nth-child( 1 ) { grid-area : head ; }
div.grid-container > div:nth-child( 2 ) { grid-area : menu ; }
div.grid-container > div:nth-child( 3 ) { grid-area : main ; }
div.grid-container > div:nth-child( 4 ) { grid-area : aside ; }
div.grid-container > div:nth-child( 5 ) { grid-area : foot ; }
```

6 Then, add rules to position each named area
```
div.grid-container { grid-template-areas :
  'head head head head head'
  'menu main main main aside'
  'menu foot foot foot foot' ; }
```

7 Save the HTML document once more, then refresh the browser to see the grid areas positioned

Hot tip

You could, alternatively, assign an **id** in the HTML elements for selection of each grid item element you wish to name.

Hot tip

Un-named elements can be specified in the list of **grid-template-areas** by a "." period/full stop character.

169

Order Items

The **grid-area** shorthand property, introduced in the previous example on pages 168-169, is very powerful as it allows any grid item element to be easily reordered within a grid container – irrespective of the order in which their elements appear in the HTML code. Assigning line numbers as a "/" forward slash-separated list of line numbers to the **grid-area** property lets you choose any order.

gridorder.html

1 Create an HTML document with a division element that contains six inner divisions

```
<div class="grid-container">
  <div>One</div> <div>Two</div> <div>Three</div>
    <div>Four</div> <div>Five</div> <div>Six</div>
</div>
```

2 Add a style sheet with rules to control the web page and to make the outer division into a grid container

```
* { margin : 0 ; padding : 0 ; box-sizing : border-box ; }

div.grid-container {
    display : grid ; height : 200px ; grid-gap : 20px 50px ;
    grid-template-columns : auto auto auto ;
    border : 2px dashed DeepSkyBlue ; }
```

3 Now, add rules to specify the appearance of the grid items

```
div.grid-container > div {
    padding : 10px 30px ; background : LightBlue ;
    border : 2px solid DeepSkyBlue ; font : 1.25em sans-serif ; }
```

4 Save the HTML document, then open it in a web browser to see the default grid item order

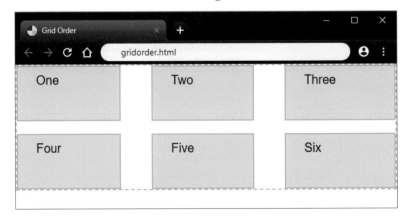

...cont'd

5 Next, add rules to change the grid items' order, then save the HTML document and refresh the browser

```
div.grid-container > div:nth-child(1) { grid-area : 1/3/2/4 ; }
div.grid-container > div:nth-child(2) { grid-area : 2/3/3/4 ; }
div.grid-container > div:nth-child(3) { grid-area : 1/1/2/2 ; }
div.grid-container > div:nth-child(4) { grid-area : 1/2/2/3 ; }
div.grid-container > div:nth-child(5) { grid-area : 2/1/3/2 ; }
div.grid-container > div:nth-child(6) { grid-area : 2/2/3/3 ; }
```

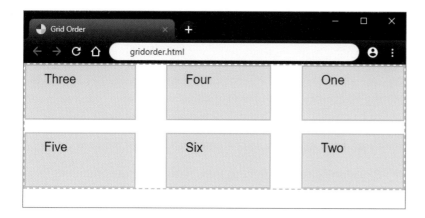

6 Finally, add rules to change the layout for small displays, then save the document and refresh/reduce the browser

```
@media screen and ( max-width:600px ) {
div.grid-container > div:nth-child(1) { grid-area : 1/span 3/2/4 ; }
div.grid-container > div:nth-child(2) { grid-area : 3/3/4/4 ; }
div.grid-container > div:nth-child(3) { grid-area : 2/1/3/2 ; }
div.grid-container > div:nth-child(4) { grid-area : 2/2/span 2/3 ; }
div.grid-container > div:nth-child(5) { grid-area : 3/1/4/2 ; }
div.grid-container > div:nth-child(6) { grid-area : 2/3/3/4 ; }
}
```

Hot tip

Notice how the **span** keyword is included here to specify relative line number coordinates.

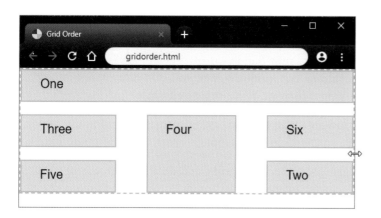

Summary

- The flexbox layout scheme is a 1-dimensional system that can wrap lines of flex items, but the grid layout scheme is a 2-dimensional system of grid items in columns and rows.

- A grid layout first requires a grid container element be created by specifying a **grid** value to its **display** property.

- The **grid-template-columns** sets the number of grid columns by specifying a space-separated list of width values.

- The **grid-template-rows** sets the number of grid rows by specifying a space-separated list of height values.

- The **auto** keyword can be specified to automatically determine the width or height of a grid column or row.

- A **justify-content** can align grid items horizontally, and an **align-items** can align grid items vertically on the line.

- An **align-content** can align lines within a grid container.

- An **align-self** can align an individual grid item selected by the **:nth-child( )** pseudo-class selector.

- The **grid-gap** is shorthand that can specify **grid-column-gap** and **grid-row-gap** additional spacing in a grid container.

- A **grid-column-start** and **grid-column-end** can specify the horizontal position and extent of a grid item.

- A **grid-row-start** and **grid-row-end** can specify the vertical position and extent of a grid item.

- The **grid-column** and **grid-row** shorthands can determine horizontal and vertical positioning by specifying two forward slash-separated values to specify start and end.

- A **grid-area** is shorthand that can specify **grid-row-start,** **grid-column-start, grid-row-end,** and **grid-column-end** by specifying a forward slash-separated list of line numbers.

- The **grid-area** property can assign names to grid items, which can be specified to **grid-template-areas** in single quote marks.

- Any grid item element can be reordered within a grid container by assigning line numbers to the **grid-area** property.

9 Design for Devices

Adapt Layouts

Web pages are viewed on a variety of devices that have different-sized display areas and different features. In fact, since 2015, more web pages are now viewed on mobile devices than desktop PCs. This means it is important that web pages are designed to look great on a variety of devices and screen sizes.

Responsive Web Design ("RWD") aims to ensure optimum usability for user satisfaction by designing web pages that present content well, and perform well, across all devices.

Web pages designed with RWD adapt their layout to suit the viewing device using only HTML and CSS – no JavaScript.

The key to Responsive Web Design is the use of CSS media queries to determine the size and capabilities of the viewing device. Having recognized the device's features, the layout can be adapted to suit the viewing environment by the use of fluid proportion-based grids and flexible images to create a responsive layout:

- **CSS Media Queries** – allow the web page to use style sheets containing rules that are appropriate for the screen size of the viewing device or width of the browser window.

- **Fluid Grid Layout** – requires the web page sizes to be specified in relative units, such as percentages and em values (rather than in absolute units such as pixel and point values), so that items can stretch or shrink.

- **Flexible Images** – requires image sizes to be specified in relative units, such as percentages, so they will not overflow their containing element on smaller viewing devices.

- **Responsive Layouts** – will automatically adapt to suit the size of the viewing device and adjust when the user resizes the browser window.

Pages optimized for Responsive Web Design <u>must</u> include the **<meta>** viewport tag in the document's head section, as described on page 12, to instruct the web browser how to control the page's dimensions and scaling. This tag's **width=device-width** value tells the browser to match the screen's width in device-independent pixels, and the tag's **initial-scale=1.0** value tells the browser to establish a 1:1 relationship between CSS pixels and device-independent pixels – irrespective of the device's orientation.

Flexible images in RWD are sometimes referred to as "context-aware".

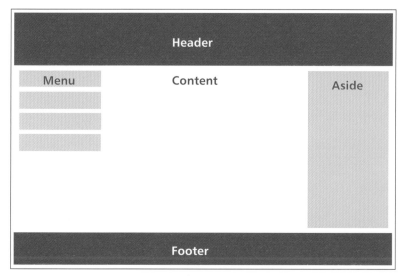

Desktop

Frequently, a Responsive Web Design will provide a 3-column web page layout for larger devices, similar to the one shown above. It will also provide a 2-column layout for medium sized devices, and a 1-column layout for smaller devices, like those shown below.

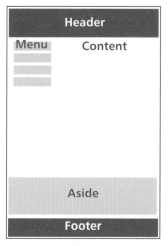

Tablet

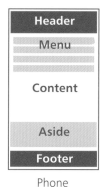

Phone

The Google Chrome web browser has a facility that lets you simulate how a web page will look on different devices. Open the web page in Google Chrome, then press the **F12** key and click the ⬜ button in the "DevTools" window to open the device toolbar in the browser window. Choose any device to simulate from the dropdown options in the device toolbar menu.

175

Looking at the layouts illustrated above it should, hopefully, be apparent that the requirements of Responsive Web Design can be satisfied using the CSS flexbox and grid layout schemes.

Compare Schemes

In deciding which layout scheme is best suited for an RWD web page design, it is useful to compare the flexbox and grid schemes.

First, recall that flexbox is intended for 1-dimensional layouts, whereas grid is intended for 2-dimensional layouts. This means that if you want to lay out items in a row, such as buttons in a horizontal navigation bar, then choose the flexbox scheme.

| Home | News | | Logout |

Conversely, if you want to lay out items in two dimensions, with both rows and columns, then choose the grid layout scheme.

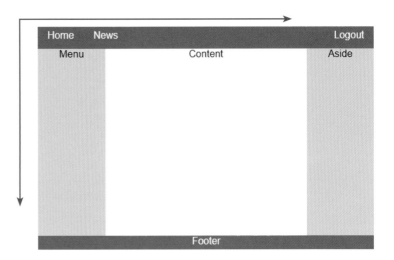

The straightforward choice of scheme for the header items in the illustrations above would then be for the flexbox layout scheme. It is, however, a useful exercise to build the header using each scheme to compare them:

flexvgrid.html

 Create an HTML document containing two similar headers, separated by a line break

```html
<header class="flex-container">
<div>Home</div><div>News</div><div>Logout</div>
</header>
<br>
<header class="grid-container">
<div>Home</div><div>News</div><div>Logout</div>
</header>
```

2 Next, add a style sheet with rules to control the page and to specify the appearance of the headers

```
* { margin : 0 ; padding : 0 ; box-sizing : border-box ; }
header { background : Tomato ; color : White ;  }
header > div { font : 1em sans-serif ; padding : 0 1em ; }
```

3 Now, add rules to create a flexbox layout and position its final item at the far right

```
header.flex-container { display : flex ; }
header.flex-container > div:nth-child(3) {
                            margin : 0 0 0 auto ; }
```

4 Then, add rules to create a grid layout with ten columns, and position its final item at the far right

```
header.grid-container { display : grid ;
        grid-template-columns : repeat( 10, 1fr ) ; }
header.grid-container > div:nth-child(3) {
                            grid-column : 10 ; }
```

Hot tip

Notice that the flexbox layout easily positions the final item to the far right by adding a left margin, whereas the grid layout must explicitly place it in the 10th column of the grid.

5 Save the HTML document, then open it in a browser to see that the headers appear to be identical

177

6 Open the browser's Developer Tools, then inspect each header to see how they compare

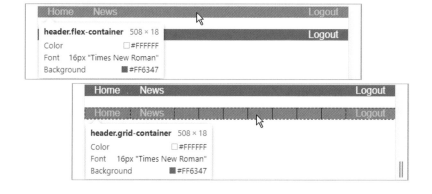

Hot tip

Open the web page in Google Chrome, then press the **F12** key and click the ⌖ button in the "DevTools" window to open the device toolbar in the browser window. Place the cursor over any element to inspect it.

Combine Schemes

The optimum solution for an RWD web page design invariably uses a combination of the grid and flexbox layout schemes. Overall page layout is best governed by grid layout and the flexbox layout is best suited for horizontal components – such as items in a navigation bar.

As more web pages are now viewed on mobile devices than desktop PCs it is good practice to design for mobile first.

responsive.html

1 Create an HTML document with a division containing header, menu, content, aside, and footer elements
```
<div class="grid-container">

    <header>
        <div>Home</div>
        <div>News</div>
        <div>Logout</div>
    </header>

    <nav>Menu</nav>
    <main>Content</main>
    <aside>Aside</aside>
    <footer>Footer</footer>

</div>
```

2 Add a style sheet with rules to control the web page and the appearance of all its text
```
* { margin : 0 ; padding : 0 ; box-sizing : border-box ;
        font : 1em sans-serif ; text-align :  center ; }
```

3 Next, add rules to specify the appearance of some page elements
```
header, footer { background : Tomato ; color : White ;  }
nav, aside { background : MistyRose ; }
```

4 Now, add rules to make the division element into a grid layout of 10 columns and 5 rows that fill the viewport
```
div.grid-container {
    display : grid ;
    width : 100vw ;
    height : 100vh ;
    grid-template-columns : repeat(10, 1fr ) ;
    grid-template-rows: 10% 15% 60% 10% 5% ;
}
```

Hot tip

The **vw** and **vh** units are viewport dimensions of 100% width and height.

5 Then, add rules to position element items in the grid

```
header  { grid-column : span 10 ; }
nav     { grid-column : span 10 ; }
main    { grid-column : span 10 ; }
aside   { grid-column : span 10 ; }
footer  { grid-column : span 10 ; }
```

6 Next, add rules to make the header element into a flexbox layout with items vertically centered

```
header { display : flex ; align-items : center ; }
```

7 Now, add rules to pad each side of the flexbox header items and position its final item at the far right

```
header > div { padding : 0 1em ; }
header > div:nth-child(3) { margin : 0 0 0 auto ; }
```

8 Save the HTML document then open it in a browser to see the combined layouts

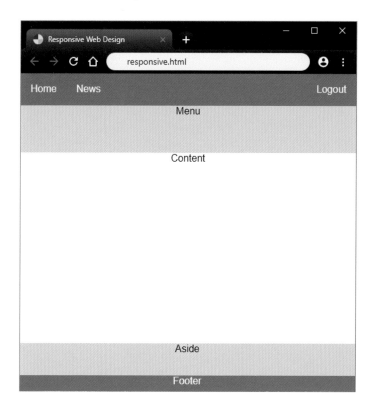

Hot tip

Adjust the size of the browser window horizontally and vertically to see the grid layout and flexbox layout are both maintained.

Add Breakpoints

The responsive web page created on pages 178-179 can now be made to adapt its layout for devices that have larger display areas by adding media queries to the style sheet. These will change the grid layout from the 1-column web page layout for small devices to a 2-column layout for medium-sized devices, and a 3-column layout for large devices.

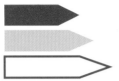

breakpoints.html

1 Make a new copy of the "responsive.html" document from page 179 and save it as "breakpoints.html"

2 In the style sheet, after the existing rules, add a media query for medium-sized devices with rules to change the layout by decreasing the number of rows from five to four

```
@media screen  and ( min-width:600px )
              and ( max-width:992px ) {

        div.grid-container {
        grid-template-rows : 10% 75% 10% 5% ; }

        nav      { grid-column : span 2 ; }
        main     { grid-column : span 8 ; }
}
```

3 Next, add another media query to change the layout for large devices by decreasing the number of rows from five to three

```
@media screen  and ( min-width:992px ) {

        div.grid-container {
        grid-template-rows : 10% 85% 5% ; }

        nav      { grid-column : span 2 ; }
        main     { grid-column : span 6 ; }
        aside    { grid-column : span 2 ; }
}
```

4 Now, save the HTML document, then open it in a variety of devices to see how the breakpoints adapt the layout

...cont'd

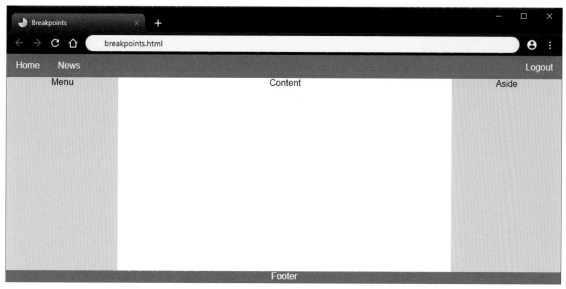

Desktop

Tablet

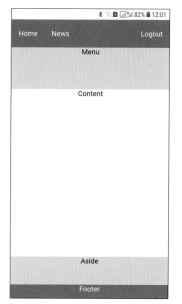

Phone

Scale Images

Responsive Web Design should recognize that images and video content on a web page should also adapt to suit viewing devices of different size.

Background images can be made to scale down and maintain their aspect ratio between width and height, by specifying the **contain** keyword to the **background-size** property and the **no-repeat** keyword to the **background-repeat** property – for example:

```
div {
          width : 100% ;
          height : 400px ;
          background-image : url(ferrari.png) ;
          background-size : contain ;
          background-repeat : no-repeat ;
}
```

But this technique will only scale down the image within its containing element – its container maintains the specified height.

If the image file size is a concern, you could specify different versions of the image for different devices using media queries to provide smaller image files to small devices for better performance. Remembering to design for mobile first, initially specify a small image file for small devices, then add media queries to specify increasingly larger image files for medium-sized and large devices.

More simply, images and video can easily be made to scale up or down using CSS rules to assign their **width** property a percentage value, and by specifying the **auto** keyword to their **height** property.

scale.html

ferrari.png
800px x 400px

1 Create an HTML document containing a division element and a single image
`<img class="scale" src="ferrari.png" alt="Ferrari">`

2 Add a style sheet with rules to control the web page
`* { margin : 0 ; padding : 0 ; box-sizing : border-box ; }`

3 Now, add rules to scale the image
`img.scale { width : 100% ; height : auto ;
                    border : 5px dashed Tomato ; }`

4 Save the HTML document, then open it in different devices to see the image scale to suit the display area

...cont'd

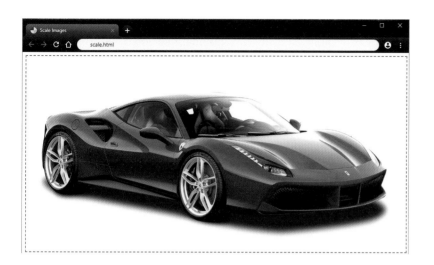

Desktop

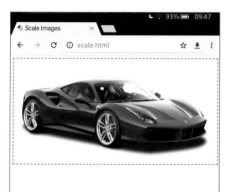

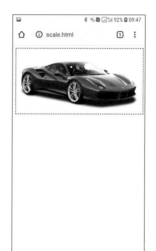

Phone

Tablet

Hide Content

CSS provides a number of ways in which web page content can be hidden from view, but with varying consequences:

- **display : none ;** – entirely removes content from the page flow, no page space reserved, and invisible to screen readers.

- **visibility : hidden ;** – remains in the page flow, page space is reserved, but content is invisible to users and screen readers.

- **opacity : 0 ;** – remains in the page flow, page space is reserved, the content is visually hidden but is visible to screen readers.

With Responsive Web Design content should, ideally, not be omitted from web pages viewed on small devices. You can, however, remove content visually from the page flow, but have it remain visible to screen readers to aid accessibility, by absolutely positioning the content outside the display area.

hidden.html

rose.png
200px x 200px

1 Create an HTML document with a division containing an image and a paragraph
```
<div class="flex-container">
<img class="rose" src="rose.png" alt="Red Rose Photo.">
<p class="screen-reader-text">The rose is the official flower of the United States of America.</p>
</div>
```

2 Add a style sheet with rules to control the web page
```
* { margin : 0 ; padding : 0 ; box-sizing : border-box ; }

body { background : Black ; }
```

3 Next, add rules to create a flexible row
```
div.flex-container {
    display : flex ;
    justify-content : center ;
}
```

4 Now, add rules to specify the appearance of the paragraph
```
p.screen-reader-text {
    font : 2em sans-serif ;
    padding : 1em ;
    color : MistyRose ;
}
```

...cont'd

5 Then, add rules to hide the paragraph on small screens and center the image
```
@media screen and ( max-width:600px ) {

        p.screen-reader-text {
        position : absolute ;
        left : -10000px ;
        width : 1px ; height : 1px ;
        overflow : hidden ;  }
}
```

Hot tip

ChromeVox is a screen reader extension for the Google Chrome browser – available from **chrome.google.com/ webstore/category/ extensions**

6 Save the HTML document then open it in a web browser and enable a screen reader

7 Drag the edge of the browser window to narrow its width – see the paragraph get hidden and the image centered

8 Click on the page to hear the screen reader read the image name and the hidden paragraph text

"Red Rose Photo. The rose is the official flower of the United States of America."

Summary

- Responsive Web Design (RWD) aims to ensure web pages present content well and perform well across all devices.

- Responsive Web Design uses media queries to determine the size and capabilities of the viewing device.

- Pages optimized for Responsive Web Design must include the **<meta>** viewport tag in the document's head section.

- Responsive Web Design requirements can be satisfied using the flexbox layout scheme and grid layout scheme.

- The flexbox layout scheme places items in rows, but the grid layout scheme places items in both rows and columns.

- The optimum solution for Responsive Web Design invariably uses a combination of the grid and flexbox layout schemes.

- It is good practice to design for mobile first, as more web pages are now viewed on mobile devices than desktop PCs.

- A responsive web page can be made to adapt its layout for devices that have larger display areas by adding media queries.

- Media queries can be used to specify different versions of an image for devices of different size.

- Background images can be made to scale down by specifying the **contain** keyword to the **background-size** property, and the **no-repeat** keyword to the **background-repeat** property.

- Images and video can be made to scale up or down by specifying a percentage value to their **width** property and the **auto** keyword to their **height** property.

- Content can be hidden and removed from the page flow by specifying the **none** keyword to the **display** property.

- The **visibility** and **opacity** properties can be used to hide content but they each reserve space on the web page.

- Content can be hidden from view and remain visible to screen readers without reserving page space by absolutely positioning the content outside the display area.